AUDITION MONOLOGS FOR STUDENT ACTORS

Selections from contemporary plays

EDITED BY
ROGER ELLIS

mp

MERIWETHER PUBLISHING
A division of Pioneer Drama Service, Inc.
Denver, Colorado

Meriwether Publishing
A division of Pioneer Drama Service, Inc.
PO Box 4267
Englewood, CO 80155

www.pioneerdrama.com

Editor: Theodore O. Zapel
Cover design: Jan Melvin

© Copyright 1999 Meriwether Publishing

Printed in the United States of America
First Edition / Hardcover ISBN: 978-1-56608-245-7

The Library of Congress has cataloged the paperback edition as follows:

Audition monologs for student actors : selections from contemporary plays   / edited and with an introduction by Gerald Lee Ratliff -- 1st ed.

    p.   cm.
    ISBN 10: 1-56608-055-2 (pbk.)
    1. Monologs. 2. Acting--Auditions.   I. Ellis, Roger. 1943-
PN2080.A885   1999
812'.04508--dc21

                                     99-37962
                                       CIP

      1   2   3   20   21   22

Acknowledgements

Among the many individuals who lent me their assistance with this book, special recognition should be given to Grand Valley State University which provided me with the much-needed funding and release time from teaching to compile and prepare the material.

I'm also grateful for the continued support and advice of my editor, Ted Zapel, at Meriwether Publishing. In addition, I'm indebted to the cooperation of numerous theatres across the nation for access to their script libraries and the help of their literary managers. Without the assistance of organizations like the Theatre Communications Group, New Dramatists, and others, several of the plays included here would not have come to my attention. Credit should also be given to all the authors' agents for their patience and cooperation in arranging permission fees and contracts with the playwrights. And last but not least I owe a debt of gratitude I can never repay to all of the actors whose performances enabled me to recognize the power and the grace, the subtlety and theatricality of the plays contained in this anthology.

Contents

Preface 1

Introduction: How to Perform Monologs 9

Actors and Monologs 9

Selecting Monologs 13

Devising the Vis-à-vis 15

Goals and Obstacles 17

Staging 18

Notes on the Monologs That Follow 21

Monologs for Women 23

Voice of the Prairie
  by John Olive 25

Retro
  by Megan Terry 27

Sea of Forms
  by Megan Terry 29

The Web
  by Martha Boesing 30

Night Luster
  by Laura Harrington 32

When the Bough Breaks
  by Robert Clyman 34

Stuck
  by Adele Edling Shank 36

Abingdon Square
  by Maria Irene Fornés 38

Wetter than Water
  by Deborah Pryor 39

The Old Settler
  by John Henry Redwood 41

Truth: The Testimonial of Sojourner Truth
  by Eric Coble 43

Nightfall With Edgar Allan Poe
  by Eric Coble 45
Sally's Gone, She Left Her Name
  by Russell Davis 47
Night Train to Bolina
  by Nilo Cruz 49
This One Thing I Do
  by Claire Braz-Valentine 51
Blue Skies Forever
  by Claire Braz-Valentine 53
Punk Girls
  by Elizabeth Wong 57
Cleveland Raining
  by Sung Rno 59
Night Breath
  by Dennis Klontz 61
The Boiler Room
  by Reuben Gonzalez 63
Interborough Transit
  by Adam Kraar 65
Lady Liberty
  by Adam Kraar 67
Who Ever Said I Was a Good Girl?
  by Gustavo Ott 69
A Tuesday in April
  by Max Bush 71
Prodigal Kiss (1)
  by Caridad Svich 73
Prodigal Kiss (2)
  by Caridad Svich 77
Jambulu
  by Mary Fengar Gail 79
The Stonewater Rapture
  by Doug Wright 81
Tongue of a Bird
  by Ellen McLaughlin 83

Monologs for Men 85

Retro
by Megan Terry 87

Sea of Forms
by Megan Terry 88

Rough Stock
by Ric Averill 89

Love's Labours Wonne
by Don Nigro 91

Abingdon Square
by Maria Irene Fornés 92

Souvenirs
by Sheldon Rosen 94

The China Crisis
by Kipp Erante Cheng 95

Final Passages
by Robert Schenkkan 97

Sunday Sermon
by David Henry Hwang 99

Principia Scriptoriae
by Richard Nelson 101

The Fifth Sun (1)
by Nicholas A. Patricca 103

The Fifth Sun (2)
by Nicholas A. Patricca 105

The Migrant Farmworker's Son
by Silvia Gonzalez S. 106

The Emerald Circle
by Max Bush 108

Heaven's Hard
by Jordan Budde 110

4 Square Blocks
by Michelle A. Hamilton 112

Les Trois Dumas
by Charles Smith 114

Brown & Black & White All Over
by Antonio Sacre 116

The Last Magician (1)
   by Albert Morell.. 119
The Last Magician (2)
   by Albert Morell.. 121
Punch Drunk
   by Ethan Sandler and Josie Dickson 123

Permissions Acknowledgements 127
About the Author 137

Preface

American Playwriting at the Turn of the Century

The Dramatists' Marketplace

One of the most startling and reliable measures of vitality in the contemporary American theatre is the staggering volume and high quality of new plays that it continues to produce. This anthology is offered as a partial reflection of some of the best new work that has been written since 1980.

Encouraged during the seventies and eighties by public and private grant monies, new American playwriting began to flourish during those decades as never before. Predictably, this development took place almost entirely on regional not-for-profit stages, although commercial theatres occasionally fed handsomely on some of its products. One thinks immediately in this regard of musicals like *RENT* or *A CHORUS LINE*, or even non-musical plays like Terence McNally's *MASTER CLASS* or Tony Kushner's *ANGELS IN AMERICA* which made successful transfers.

Surprisingly today, the number of new plays written and staged in our nation's playhouses each year dwarfs the number of new screenplays written and produced by the film industry. Today, writers' retreats, play development and writers' residency programs, new plays festivals, and commissioned works are a familiar part of the theatrical landscape. In professional and amateur settings alike, despite the economic challenges confronting all our theatres, the number of new plays seems to increase each season.

This phenomenon becomes doubly interesting when considered in light of the growing — one might even say daunting — influence of the mass media in our society. In an age when blockbuster films and television programs weekly attract hundreds of millions of patrons worldwide, the studios and media moguls still allot tens of millions in development dollars each year to promoting new work for the live stage. Dozens of graduates from university playwriting programs are prepared to trade their caps and gowns each year for lucrative jobs in Hollywood's writers' stables; while seasoned pros like José Rivera or Eric Overmyer cheerfully wave studio contracts in one hand and pen new stage plays with the other. Nor should we overlook the global media giants like Disney and Warner who invest vast sums to exploit theatre audiences and gain cultural prestige with splashy Broadway productions, cable channel theatrical specials, and digital-celluloid adaptations of Shakespeare and other stage classics.

I offer these last examples not as proof of the vitality of American playwriting (the success of *SHAKESPEARE IN LOVE* or *BEAUTY AND THE BEAST* have nothing to do with new script development); but instead as illustrations of the entertainment industry's voracious search for new creative "product" that has in turn created a new climate among theatregoers welcoming original work. The increasingly evident marriage-of-convenience between stage and screen — not just in writing — has generated, I believe, a much more receptive attitude among the public than in years past for new artistry in many contexts, including new plays for the theatre.

There are, of course, other more legitimate reasons why new American playwriting continues to develop at such a feverish pace. Chief among them, I think, is the freedom of expression that many playwrights continue to enjoy. Unfettered by the dollar-driven agendas of Hollywood executives and the accompanying formula writing that largely characterizes film and television programming for mainstream markets, playwrights are able to develop scripts for the theatre on personally important or socially sensitive themes, and in artistically challenging styles that media entertainment can never replicate. Hollywood's best shot to-date at the AIDS crisis, for example, *PHILADELPHIA*, seems sappy and anemic by comparison with a host of new plays on the same subject. The Pulitzer-winning *ANGELS IN AMERICA* is merely the tip of that iceberg. And the brilliant innovative work of playwrights like Suzanne Lori-Parks, OyamO, Paula Vogel and many others has challenged the most inventive designers, directors and producers at home and abroad to explore new forms of expression in theatrical writing.

A more abstract reason why new playwriting flourishes in the United States today is the centrality of the author in the theatrical process — a role which strongly appeals to many authors despite the theatre's marginal role and impact today by comparison with pop films and TV. Unlike the solitary and often marginalized work of the poet or novelist, or the frustration of screenwriters at the bottom of Hollywood's food chain, the writer is still universally respected in the playhouse. And in the arena of new plays, the writer is certainly the most active participant in the production process. All signs seem to indicate that in the twenty-first century, hack writers will continue to find easy employment in many areas of the communications and entertainment industries; but for serious authors with something to express, the live stage promises the writer a respected role at the center of the action.

Playwrights and Social Issues

The work of emerging playwrights intent on using the stage as a forum for social problems has also fueled new play development in the United States. Our theatrical pantheon abounds with new writers centering their sights upon themes of racism, immigration, media violence, prison reform, gender stereotyping, political oppression and similar domestic issues. Migdalia Cruz, David Henry Hwang, August Wilson, Anna Deveare Smith, Eduardo Machado, Diana Son — these and many others find theatre a more accessible medium for cogent argument and analysis than mainstream film and television with their disappointing restrictions of self-censorship that are often enforced by "designer-driven" marketing strategies.

Oddly enough, the very same dollars that account for the talent drain luring writers from the stage to Hollywood seems to explain why so many new playwrights turn to the theatre as their medium-of-choice: it's affordable and relatively free of the competitive greed and excess that seem to characterize so much of the entertainment industry. After all, no one embarks on a theatre career in order to get rich. And of course, for women and writers-of-color, the stage offers an opportunity to develop themes and characters free of the gender and racial stereotyping that seems to dominate much of our society's mass media. This anthology contains a number of such writers. Some of them are well-established theatrical names like David Henry Hwang, Maria Irene Fornés, and Richard Nelson; while others such as Eric Coble, Kipp Erante Cheng, or John Henry Redwood are more recent arrivals upon the theatrical scene.

Socially-concerned authors today, though, do not necessarily restrict themselves to ethnic or racial issues. Some writers represented in this collection have indeed made their mark as "ethnic voices" dealing with problems of racism in much of their work, such as Silvia Gonzalez S., Sung Rno, and Caridad Svich. But others of them take aim at international cultural issues such as Mary Fengar Gail's and Sheldon Rosen's critiques of western cultural imperialism. Max Bush deals

3

frequently in his plays with the problems of American teenagers. A number of female playwrights included here speak powerfully to the concerns of women, such as Martha Boesing's critique of male-dominated literary criticism in *THE WEB*, or Adele Edling Shank's commentary on sexual exploitation of women in *STUCK*. Other authors like Gustavo Ott or Michelle A. Hamilton take aim at the problems of urban violence, while still others examine the issue of human rights on a global scale such as Nilo Cruz's poignant description of the plight of refugee children in *NIGHT TRAIN TO BOLINA*.

Playwrights and History

Of special note among new American playwrights are those who tend to focus on the historical roots of social problems instead of concerning themselves exclusively with the contemporary symptoms of social malaise. They deepen and extend our understanding of ourselves by directing attention to the past for clues to our present situation and problematic future. This penchant for history, of course, has been one of the drama's strongest sources of inspiration from Graeco-Roman times through the Renaissance, and up to the present day; it is encouraging to observe how powerful a strain it still remains in the contemporary theatre.

Chief among this group of authors found in this anthology are Nicholas A. Patricca's analysis of Central American political corruption in *THE FIFTH SUN*, or Charles Smith's critique of state racism in *LES TROIS DUMAS*. Don Nigro's discussion of the loss of spiritual values in modern society is marvelously expressed in his play on Shakespeare, *LOVE'S LABOURS WONNE*, while Albert Morell treats the same subject in a nineteenth-century context with his drama on Aleister Crowley.

Playwrights dealing with the social history of the United States are also represented here. Feminist historical perspectives can be found in Claire Braz-Valentine's *BLUE SKIES FOREVER*, a portrait of Amelia Earhart, and *THIS ONE THING I DO* which portrays the work of Susan B. Anthony and Elizabeth Cady Stanton. Such plays as Eric Coble's *TRUTH: THE TESTIMONIAL OF SOJOURNER TRUTH*, John Olive's *VOICE OF THE PRAIRIE*, and Robert Schenkkan's *FINAL PASSAGES* are other examples of how contemporary playwrights continue to find "Americana" a fertile source of new ideas and important personal and public insight.

Editorial Considerations

My purpose in selecting the monologs for this anthology has been twofold: I've tried to highlight some of the most interesting scripts written for the American theatre over the past two decades, and in so doing to provide a resource for readers, teachers, and theatre professionals looking to contemporary playwrights for new insight, new material for competitions and studio work, and new possibilities for productions.

Because of the limited exposure audiences and readers have to the range and variety of new dramatic writing taking place in many regions of the United States, there seems a great need to gather together some of the most important work being done in this field, and make it more accessible to the public. For this reason, I've tried to fix my attention on plays largely unavailable in published form, although some of these works — especially those by established writers — may be familiar to avid playgoers. And all the scripts in this anthology have received some type of public response, either in the form of staged readings or even fully mounted productions, which is always indispensable for developing new work for the theatre.

Of special concern to me, however, has been the suitability of these monologs for educational purposes. Hence, I've tried to include only those pieces with characters able to be played by young actors between fifteen and twenty-five years of age. My hope in doing so has been that the book should serve the special needs of high school and university teachers. I've also tried to focus on plays containing themes of interest to this age group. Some of the dramas have been specifically written for young audiences such as THE EMERALD CIRCLE by Max Bush, and THE MIGRANT FARMWORKER'S SON by Silvia Gonzalez S. However, readers will soon discover that the majority of these plays have been written for general audiences, although the monologs here contain themes or characters especially appropriate for younger students.

As previously discussed, I've also tried to remain sensitive to considerations of gender and ethnic diversity when making editorial decisions. A number of controversial women writers are included here, as well as female characters both young and old, contemporary and historical. In the category of ethnic diversity, I've sought to include representative writers and characters from Hispanic, African-American and Asian backgrounds in order to reflect the increasing cultural pluralism both in our schools and in society at large. Although this group of socially-concerned writers are often accused of introducing

5

problematic and explosive treatments of gender or racial issues, I've tried to keep the anthology free of vulgar language and strictly adult situations, while still retaining the playwright's incisive treatment of the subject at hand.

I have done little or no editing of any of the pieces, except to remove them from the context of the entire play. All the extracts in the book have been reviewed and approved by the authors. One of the collection's most interesting features, however, is the variety in length of the selections. None of the monologs here are shorter than ninety seconds, and some may stretch to several minutes in length. Students and coaches preparing for competitive auditions — scholarships, casting, forensics competitions, etc. — might therefore need to cut their pieces to a required length. On the other hand, I should remind readers that the printed length of a monolog is never a good indication of its performance length, which always depends on the number of heartbeats in the monolog — not the number of words. The monologs should therefore be read aloud if only to judge their length, and the potential emotional power they contain.

A Reminder About Intellectual Property

In all the anthologies I edit, I feel compelled to remind readers that the monologs in the collection are intended only for studio exercises or for reading. When it comes to performing them, producing them in public readings, or adapting them in any way via the electronic media for other audiences — educational, amateur, or professional — then permission must be obtained and royalties paid to the agent or author.

Perhaps this "caution" needs to be restated in this age of the Internet where so much is available online or otherwise reproducible at little or no charge. Readers must remind themselves that plays — like other unique, cultural artifacts — are not equivalent to the bytes and "factoids" we slug through and manipulate by the thousands every day. They are the intellectual property of human beings who have spent many years earning, and who therefore deserve, proper acknowledgment and compensation for producing and distributing them to the public.

Bear in mind that I'm attempting in this book to highlight and promote the work of a handful of uniquely talented and very highly motivated artists whose worth, importance and cultural value in our society is already deeply discounted, frequently ridiculed, and even despised. Their plays are their honest work, their "products." Pay for them. If you wish to perform any of these monologs in public, credits appear at the end of this volume; call or write for permission. These artists are not unreasonable in what they expect from us.

Introduction:
How to Perform Monologs

Actors and Monologs

I've always felt that one of the worst burdens imposed on actors today is the demand that they audition with monologs. The monolog is now enshrined as part of the actor's equipment, just as essential as a resumé, a union card or an 8 x 10 glossy. Students must perform them for scholarship and entrance competitions, stock performers must run them by producers in thirty-to-sixty second fragments at massive cattle calls, while other professionals must often deliver them to overworked and unsympathetic casting directors in offices or rehearsal halls or unfamiliar theatre stages.

Suddenly, that is, this administrative convenience of the dramatic monolog has become elevated to the status of the sink-or-swim entrance requirement for finding work in plays and often in film and television. It is, after all, only an administrative convenience that directors require monologs at all. It would be totally unrealistic and impractical to expect every actor to bring along a friend for each audition in order to perform in a two-character scene. And so the monolog is used instead as a convenient device for initially screening actors when casting plays.

The problem is that every one of us — directors, actors, coaches, producers — frequently place too much weight upon this solo performance, or mistake its value in a casting situation. Actors, for example, often feel they must provide the character which is being sought (as if they're expected to read the auditors' minds!); or they must "blow the casting people out of the room" with their monolog performance in order to get noticed; or they feel they should cram as much "technique" as possible into their performance so the directors will know they're skilled and they've been trained.

On the other side of the table, casting people most frequently fall into the trap of expecting these kinds of misguided monolog performances, and accepting them as more or less "final." Instead of seeking actors who might be able to develop a role, auditors tend to look for "type," for finished products. There is no time. The "right" person is out there. The pressure of the casting situation prods directors and actors to rely over much upon the monolog performance as the main indicator of who is the right actor to play the role.

All these confusions (and more) muddy the waters of the casting situation, especially for actors. Not knowing exactly what the directors are looking for — even if you've been fortunate enough to read the script — you're left with a host of contradictory choices in selecting and performing your monolog. Here are a few that have always plagued me:

"Are they looking for the traditional character, the straight character? Do they want the correct interpretation of the speech at this moment of the play?"

"Can I get some inside information on what the directors are looking for in order to shape my performance better?"

"Are they looking for my potential as an actor, regardless of the monolog I choose? or the way I choose to interpret it?"

"Should I select a monolog from the play being cast? If I do will I run up against the director's fixed notion of whom he or she wants to see in the part?"

"Will the directors be comparing me with actors they've seen in the part before? or earlier today? Should I therefore use a totally original monolog? or do something offbeat?"

"Do I need to score an impression with something bold and physical? or something with a lot of explosive emotions in order to earn a callback?"

"Does this monolog really show them the range of my abilities? Can I "push" the monolog in order to do this? Is the monolog appropriate for the part (whatever it is)?"

It's almost as though you feel yourself part of some cookie-cutter process frantically caught up in the casting maze. You're trying to outguess the auditors as you decide which cartoon character type they're supposedly looking for.

But alas! The monolog is here to stay and we all learn to deal with it. Since the time when George Abbott began requiring auditions monologs, we've grown used to it as another feature of doing business in this business we love. Yet despite all this confusion about monologs, there's much that you can do to improve your performance of them in competitive situations.

First of all, monolog workshops are offered in many cities, mainly by professional theatres. Unfortunately there are only two books available on the subject, mine and Michael Shurtleff's; so it would be hard to simply "teach yourself" without coaching of some kind. Taking workshops, therefore, is an excellent way to improve your performance. Attending auditions as frequently as you can is another excellent way to build your confidence and get used to the audition situation (nothing counts like experience in this area, believe me!). Finally, performing your monologs for teachers, coaches, and other actors can also give you confidence, keep your skills sharp, and give you lots of good suggestions for how to improve yourself.

But before you run off and do any of this, there's one fundamental point I want to stress: a monolog can and should only be used to demonstrate an actor's potential for a role. Yes, of course, the auditors are looking for the "right" actor to come along. But actors always make a big mistake by thinking that the monolog can supply that magical pre-fabbed "character" who will fill the director's bill. Never aim at "character" in your monolog, aim only at honest responses to the dramatic situation. You can never know what exactly a director will be seeking, or what will turn a director off, so it's useless to try. And it's a big mistake to think of substituting a posture, an attitude, or a "character" for the emotional truth you've created and rehearsed.

Of course there are always directors who lack the time or the ability to look at an auditionee carefully. Frequently they're just trying to save themselves rehearsal work by finding an actor ready-made for the role. These kinds of directors lack confidence in their abilities to coach an actor successfully through rehearsals in order to develop a role. We must suffer such people — and they are numerous, believe me, especially in film and television — because they give us work from time to time.

If you're lucky enough to be the type they're looking for, well and good. But don't try to stuff your original, unique self into some preconceived mold for the sake of a director who thinks he or she knows exactly what's called for. Most successful actors in auditions have shown directors dimensions to the role that they never conceived of beforehand; and directors who deny this are frequently rewarded with an opening night performance hardly different from the auditions.

When an actor "goes for type" in this way he or she has abandoned the one thing which can make the audition performance absolutely vital, special and authentic: his or her own personality. Instead, the actor is left only with a simplification, a reduction of the role, an abstract idea which is supposed to fit the mold. You can't play an abstraction with any degree of interest, it's the kiss of death at an audition. You must respond in truthful ways to the emotional circumstances in which the character finds herself or himself. That's what acting is all about — not living up to the expectations of a director, teacher, or agent.

The following suggestions for preparing monologs are all based on this belief that a good monolog audition, like any good acting performance, is never forgotten. Though you may not be right for the play or film or commercial this time, you'll certainly score a strong impression in the auditors' memories. Producers and directors have told me this many times, and they've also stressed how quickly they eliminate from consideration actors who "act all over the place," as though "technique" or "character" were theatrically interesting. They're not, and I know I'm not the only actor who's received a call months after I've been turned down for one role — only to learn that the director remembered my acting and called me back to read for another part he was casting somewhere else.

For this reason I make my students in monolog classes refer to *themselves* in the situation and not to "the character." The temptation to throw up and hide behind a character is always deadly. Actors must learn instead to embody the character and experience the dramatic situation as fully as possible.

So in the suggestions which follow, remember always to place yourself in the circumstances of the role and avoid as much as possible distancing yourself from it, intellectually or emotionally. Avoid analyzing or explaining your monolog in terms like: "My character is..." or "My character feels..." Always use yourself: "I am" or "I feel." As the great Stanislavski said about this "magic if" of acting: "Remove yourself from the plane of acting, and place yourself instead on the plane of your own human emotions."

12

Monologs then must at all times be a vehicle for revealing yourself, your responses in the character's situation. If the casting people are looking for a strong type, you can never know what that means to them. It's silly to worry about it because you'll either fit the type or you won't. What can and will interest them at all times is authentic, vital and impassioned acting, and a stereotype can never be as authentic as your own deeply felt emotional truth.

So have enough confidence in yourself to respond with all the richness and truth of a human being's emotional and intellectual life to the problems the monolog presents, instead of acting what you think the auditors want to see. Your personalization of the dramatic material will always reveal a more interesting, more compelling human being than any lifeless character type. Acting honestly is the necessary first step along the path that leads to a successful monolog performance.

Selecting Monologs

I've called this book "audition monologs" because all the pieces I've selected are specifically suited to the competitive situation of auditioning. This sets the collection apart from so many other monolog anthologies on the market which are little more than collections of long speeches taken from plays. Though these monolog books are frequently an actor's first step in finding material to use for an audition, it's important to remember that most of them are assembled by people who have no particular skill or experience in auditioning as actors. Hence those books often lack the special features that distinguish speeches in plays from monologs that are well-suited for auditions.

What are those special features? What are the drawbacks of monologs that are simply lifted more or less verbatim from playscripts? One of them is the fact that a character in a play who speaks at length in a monolog might simply be "talking to himself" at that point in the action: calmly going over some of the events in the plot or making observations about other characters. Also many speeches which do contain strong emotions usually occur at a point where the performance has already gained strong momentum prior to the character's finding herself or himself alone On-stage for a few moments. Finally, many speeches you'll find in plays often discuss subjects from a nostalgic standpoint because the character is reminiscing about an incident or situation.

None of these qualities will help you in an audition, and too often I see these long speeches performed by high school students in scholarship auditions or in forensics contests. A monolog aimed at commenting upon or recounting the plot of a play is likely to be useless and dull to directors casting a different show. And even if those circumstances do yield strong emotional responses, it often takes awhile to build up to them. In an audition you don't have that time to "work into" your piece, to build up emotional momentum the way a play does in performance. Your monolog must be vital and compelling from the outset because directors are often listening only for the first fifteen seconds. Finally, nostalgic and reminiscent monologs simply lack the emotional energy that you need to propel yourself On-stage for a strong audition.

Many speeches taken verbatim from plays work well in the context of that play's production, but not all of them are specifically aimed at presenting a human being grappling with important problems, and in need of communicating that experience to someone here and now. This is the main thing that makes a good audition monolog.

The best monologs I've witnessed (acting abilities aside) have been those pieced together from a two-character scene. Here the character is already involved in a strong give-and-take of ideas with others. He or she is aggressively struggling for communication and victory in getting what he or she wants from the other character. With that other character edited out of the scene, the actor is able to piece together a single monolog from bits and pieces of dialog.

With such material you give the auditors the chance to see a much wider range of your talent as you develop from beginning to end in the scene. You use the other character's lines as springboards, as your motivation for different reactions and different obstacles to overcome. This forces you to play constantly changing actions in response to them. I bring this up to stress the fact that there must always be other characters On-stage with you, characters with whom you have strong emotional relationships as you deliver the speech.

Not all actors are good playwrights, however. Editing together a series of shorter speeches into a single consistent situation with a beginning-middle-end is not an easy task. And writing your own monolog is always a no-no (unless you're as good a writer as Lanford Wilson, Wendy Wasserstein, Arthur Miller or others). Nor are actors familiar with a wide variety of recent scripts from which to choose — especially scripts containing characters within their age range. Perhaps for this reason alone, monolog anthologies are handy, popular choices for actors. But you'll finds that all the pieces included here do possess that fundamental quality of a good audition piece: they present characters grappling with problems, characters who feel an urgent need to communicate that need to someone else.

Some of these monologs have been taken intact from plays, others have been pieced together from a series of shorter pieces with the lines of the other character edited out. What's important is that you concentrate upon that need to communicate in a relationship even though you're the only actor On-stage. It is relationship that underlies every bit of acting you will ever do, and it must form the basis of single-character speeches just as it lies at the heart of multiple-character scenes.

Devising the Vis-à-vis

"Vis-à-vis" is the technical term for the other (imaginary) character to whom you're speaking. Michael Shurtleff, the nation's most successful acting coach, recommends that you "bring a friend On-stage with you so it won't seem so lonely for you up there during your dreadful little monolog." What he means is that you must have someone up there whom you're trying to influence in order for the monolog to work as it should. Without this other character On-stage resisting, attacking, rejecting, or even ignoring you, then your performance will tend to be limp and flaccid, unfocused and lacking in energy.

Now it's not always possible to know exactly who your listener actually is. Some of your monologs, of course, have been taken from scenes in which the listener(s) is well defined. For example, Katherina's famous speech at the conclusion of Shakespeare's *TAMING OF THE SHREW* is spoken to the wedding guests. But other situations may not be so familiar, and that's when you must be creative and invent a good listener. The monologs in this book are like that: they're all taken from recent plays which might be difficult, and in many cases, impossible, for you to find and read. So you'll have to invent a good listener for yourself.

If you can read the whole play before auditioning with a monolog, then well and good. But it really isn't necessary for you to do so in order to do a good "cold reading" of material with which you're unfamiliar. You can familiarize yourself with the "given circumstances" suggested in the speech itself (a process of close reading and imagination), and then add emotional responses from your own personal experiences that are analogous to those of the character (a process of improvisation and substitution).

Normally you'll find that your monolog will give you some indication of who your listener is, but this may be only minimal, and in any case it's not your own choice — something that may work well for you at this audition. Make your vis-à-vis work for you in the performance by investing him or her with some personal attributes from your own life. We call this "substitution" because it involves substituting people, emotions or problems from your own life for those you find in the play. It helps you identify more easily and quickly with the relationship you're playing.

Whether you invent the vis-à-vis and the reasons why you must speak the monolog to him or her, or whether you deduce those things from the script itself, is unimportant. What only matters is that you commit to the goal you're trying to accomplish, the victory you're trying to win from that other character. The auditors will never know what personal stimuli you're using to energize the speech. They'll only be concerned with the intensity and believability of your acting. This is why the proper choice of vis-à-vis can be enormously helpful to you in an audition.

I always advise students to pick an imaginary listener who is unsympathetic to the character's needs and desires (your needs and desires). This will guarantee that there's conflict in the scene, and will force you to fight strongly for what you want. Stop for a moment and think of the most famous monologs and soliloquies ever written those from Jonson, Shakespeare, Molière and others. Conflict is always up front in those speeches.

Although they appear to be alone, no character is ever truly alone On-stage. Hamlet, for example, is really talking to others during his soliloquies: to his mother (who has cheapened herself by marrying Claudius), to Ophelia (who continues to hit on him despite his feigned madness), to his dead father (who continually whips him on to vengeance), or to his wicked stepfather (who has stolen Hamlet's crown, murdered Hamlet's dad, and parties-down in the palace while mocking and threatening Hamlet). This is what makes those soliloquies vital, compelling and dramatic.

You must create this same kind of demanding vis-à-vis for yourself. Use someone from your own life because then you can see that person On-stage playing opposite you. Place him or her Down-stage of you (so you'll always be "open" to the auditors). Visualize specific reactions of that person to your words. Imagine him or her trying to walk out on you, ignore you, hit you, mock you, protest to you, etc. Use those reactions to reinforce your acting moment-by-moment in the monolog. Create a vivid relationship with your vis-à-vis and you'll add tremendous vitality to your monolog.

This other character should also be someone who is especially important to you, whose opinions and actions you need and respect. This person can be an enemy (Hamlet's Claudius is a "bloody, bawdy, damnable villain."), or a friend. (Hamlet's Ophelia is a gorgeous, passionate, and understanding female.) Frequently the best listeners are those like Ophelia — or like your family members — with whom you have a love-hate relationship. Anything is better in a vis-à-vis than complacency, ordinariness or indifference which is too often seen in monolog auditions. All that matters for your audition is that you absolutely commit yourself to winning over your vis-à-vis.

If you make the stakes of your conflict high enough then your acting will become more vigorous and interesting to the director. The vis-à-vis should therefore be a character who is the only one capable of providing whatever it is that you need to turn your life around and win happiness. Your character's problem — your problem — is not something that can be overcome by mundane solutions to mundane questions that anyone can offer. Only this vis-à-vis can do it for you, only this dramatic moment offers life-or-death importance to you. Anything less is dull acting.

Goals and Obstacles

Many coaches say that an ability to understand and play strong goals and obstacles in a scene lies at the heart of good acting. An actor who knows — or who gives the audience the impression that he or she knows — what he or she wants in a scene, is an actor who will compel our attention and create a riveting relationship for us. Think about it: in life (as on the stage), when you know you want something desperately, completely, absolutely, then you'll engage in any conflict and devise any tactics to get it. Right? That's why identifying or inventing strong, clear, and concrete goals for your character is one-half the battle you've got to win. The other one-half is in finding out or inventing what it is about your vis-à-vis that prevents you from winning.

Your goal in a monolog can never be something single, it must always be multiple in order for your "character" to develop, to change, and thereby hold our interest. (When did you ever struggle in order to end up in the same place you started?) In life we never get what we want without overcoming obstacles: other drivers on the freeway, greedy ex-wives, domineering parents, rivals in love, etc. And in each encounter with these "others" there will be a number of things we want from that other person. In fact, we often discover them in the course of the encounter, because of the encounter.

Of course, this always happens in two-character scenes where the "beats" change as the scene develops. But remember that you're treating the monolog as a two-character scene — something with a vis-à-vis — for auditioning purposes. So in the speech you should examine the lines for what your character seeks and what stands in your way. If it's not indicated in the monolog then you must invent or improvise your own. Don't worry about embarrassing yourself because your invention might be too "personal." The audience will never know what your goals and obstacles are; they'll just note that your acting is vital and compelling.

These different goals should be clear to you moment-by-moment as you perform your monolog. You should attack each of them strongly when they occur in the speech for variety, contrast and pace. Uta Hagen, one of this country's most respected actresses and teachers, remarks that this is one of the most valuable things an actor can do in a monolog: playing the pattern of actions that will give shape, development and clarity to the speech. What you want in the scene will change as your vis-à-vis presents various obstacles to counter each of your goals, forcing you to adopt new goals and tactics to get what you want.

So use your vis-à-vis in two ways: as a person from whom you need something vital, and as someone who continually denies you the satisfaction you crave. This will help to intensify your performance by deepening the relationship between you. You'll create and define that relationship much more effectively by playing these patterns of goals and obstacles during your performance.

Staging

Remember that the kind of acting you do in an audition will always differ from acting in a play performance because an audition requires vitality and urgency right from the outset. You must compel the auditors' attention, curiosity and interest during the first few moments. Directors usually make crucial decisions about your abilities from the way you take the stage and introduce yourself even before you think you're "acting." A cliché that is nonetheless true is that directors often reach a decision about you in the first fifteen seconds of the audition.

Most of the monologs in this anthology provide opportunities for good strong acting choices right from the outset of the speech, and you must rehearse to play these strongly. Again, some monologs give clear indications of such choice in the lines, while others require that you invent your own circumstances not only throughout the speech but especially at the beginning.

I can't say too much about this need to kick off your audition with energy and drive. Most actors already know you must "get your best up front" and "lead with your strengths," either on a resumé or at an audition. Many actors have their own personal methods of doing this in performance. Sometimes the motivation for "attacking" your piece strongly at the beginning is actually built into the speech, or in the given circumstances of the speech or scene. Obviously during the performance of an entire play this sort of motivation is part of the actor's consistent "through line" to his or her role. But remember that in an audition you lack such emotional momentum to bank upon. You simply enter, make your introduction to the auditors, and then — bang! — it's showtime and you're on!

So I believe you need more than just the given circumstances of the play or monolog to accomplish the audition kickoff effectively. No matter how compelling your character's situation may seem in dramatic terms, those terms are really not your own, they are the play's. What you need as an actor is something else, some personal trigger for your emotional commitment that can propel you into the first few moments of your audition piece.

Actors do this most frequently by using what Stanislavski called "emotional memory." All of us have a wealth of intense emotional experience in our past lives. Often we repress such knowledge because it's painful: memories of death or loss, the breakup of a love relationship, an accident which occurred to you or a loved one. On the other hand, we frequently call to mind the intense positive memories and feelings. Is there anyone who hasn't daydreamed or "replayed scenarios" of those happy times in order to imaginatively relive them? Moments of victory in a ballgame, the thrill and tingle of that first kiss with someone special, the delight in receiving a long-awaited message or gift? We often cherish such experiences in our waking fantasies for years after they originally occurred; and invariably they carry along with them many related sensory impressions: the fragrance of cologne, the chill of the autumn air, the bright colors of the ballgame, and so on. You need these kinds of vivid images in order to energize the monolog from the opening moments.

You can evoke these feelings in yourself very easily by finding a key word or image that serves as an instant trigger for recalling the experience. In everyday life isn't this how it often happens? The sound of a familiar tune, a casual remark by someone, the discovery of some long-forgotten keepsake — and suddenly we're plunged into the sadness or the fear once again, the ecstasy of remembrance or the thrill of expectation. Indeed, it often seems more intense in recollection than it was at the time. Actors frequently do this in order to cry On-stage, to register shock, joy or fear.

So once you've rehearsed other aspects of your monologs, look to add this kind of inciting action at the opening in order to be "on" from the very first. An unmistakable kiss of death in an audition is an actor taking forever to "get in character" before starting, while the directors lose interest and curiosity with each dismal second that passes. And then to have the actor slowly drift into the piece as he or she gradually works up some excitement. By that time, of course, the auditors are usually sending out for coffee, leafing through their notes of prior auditionees, or fumbling under their seats for dropped pencils. They let you continue perhaps out of courtesy or because something might eventually "happen" as you drone on in the background. But most of the time you're only just digging yourself out of the grave you created in the opening emotionless moments.

Most people who understand little about acting hold very different views about how their emotions function. In short, they're victims of their emotions. They don't believe that emotion can — or should — be turned on and off like a faucet because there's something arbitrary, dishonest, phoney about that in "real" life. As an actor, though, you must be more in touch with and more in control of your emotional life than ordinary people are. You must understand that the emotional "truth" of a dramatic situation can be communicated to an audience by a variety of methods — and often without your feeling anything (except perhaps stage fright!).

So with this final suggestion to energize the opening moments of your monolog performance, look for those personal associations and key words and images that will trigger the strong feeling you need to get out On-stage with focus and purpose. It's useful and necessary in every audition. And who knows? If your emotional memory contains an experience analogous or even identical to that of your character, then so much the better. It sometimes happens.

Good luck with the monologs that follow. And keep in mind that the prefatory remarks that accompany them are only suggestions for you. They're simply things to consider, handy departure points for the unique choices you should make in order to create a vital, compelling relationship On-stage with your vis-à-vis.

Notes on the Monologs That Follow

Most of the monologs can be performed within a two-minute limit, and some can be condensed as short as one minute. A few longer selections have been selected for class or studio work, but these have been selected with an eye on their possibilities for cutting. If you feel you must cut, then lines should be edited out internally rather than by simply lopping off the beginning or ending of a selection.

Where a monolog specifically requires an actor of an ethnic background, this has been indicated. Most of the pieces, though, are suitable for performers of any ethnic background. And don't confine yourself to looking only at those pieces indicated for your gender. It's not unusual to find that a selection originally written for the opposite sex can work well for you.

The age range indicated at the top of each selection is only a rough guide, although in most cases it does follow the age of the character in the original script. Bear in mind, though, that the age of any dramatic character is not necessarily the same as the actor's chronological age: "range" means what an actor is physically and emotionally capable of playing with believability.

The designations "comic/serious/seriocomic" are also suggestions and you should not feel absolutely constrained to adhere to these guidelines.

I sometimes use the terms "ladder" and "stepping stone" in describing a particular monolog. A "ladder" type of speech is one which builds more or less steadily from beginning to end (sometimes called a "climactic" speech because it gradually rises to an emotional climax). The stepping-stone monolog instead creates emotional peaks at various points according to different stimuli within the speech. Its highest emotional point may sometimes occur at or near the end, but it can't be played effectively as a straightforward, gradual build in intensity. Learning how to identify and play the high points in a speech is the key here.

MONOLOGS
FOR WOMEN

The Voice of the Prairie
by John Olive

1   Frances – 28   Female – Serious
2
3   *Beneath the apparently quiet surface of these words lies a*
4   *depth of feeling that presents rich opportunities to the actor.*
5   *Frances has a strong desire to communicate with her vis-à-vis*
6   *and to explain the unique way in which she sees the world.*
7   *There's also much quiet humor or amusement, as well as*
8   *profound sadness, admiration, puzzlement and curiosity in*
9   *the piece. It's one of those rare monologs that permits an actor*
10   *to develop to the full whatever emotional range she possesses*
11   *and is skilled at presenting.*
12
13   I don't know what life is. And that's what life is. I said
14   that to James and he was so upset, he couldn't even
15   pray. James prays hard. I love him when he prays, he's
16   like a tea kettle, just before it boils. Have you ever had
17   a wonderful dream, or a horrible dream for that matter,
18   and it leaves you with a feeling that you absolutely must
19   tell someone about it, but when you try, you can't
20   remember? That's what life is. So I try not to think
21   about it. It's all just dreams, and what are dreams
22   worth? James says we live only for the life to come, and
23   everything else is worthless. The devil lives in the past.
24   Don't think about it, he says. But these voices from the
25   past, these ... phantoms and demons of my imagination,
26   whatever they are, they shriek at me. Sometimes, I can't
27   hear anything else. I try to tell James. But he just
28   weeps, and prays, then goes for long walks and comes
29   back all sweaty, then his asthma acts up, and his voice

1   squeaks, and I laugh, and then it starts all over again. I
2   can't help it. I'm terrible. I'm a very highly regarded
3   member of my community. Everyone thinks the world of
4   me. I've been written up in a number of publications. I'm
5   the only blind schoolteacher in the entire state of
6   Arkansas. I'm an inspiration to them all. The street I live
7   on is dreamy and quiet, filled with honeysuckle,
8   bougainvillea, freesia, a layer cake of fragrances. That's
9   what life should be. Well. You should understand, of
10   course, that to me the world looks like this.
11
12
13
14
15
16
17
18
19
20
21
22
23
24
25
26
27
28
29
30
31
32
33
34
35

Retro
by Megan Terry

1   Mira – 29   Hispanic Female – Serious
2

3   *Every actor should enjoy this piece which describes Mira's*
4   *elation at her successful audition, and the consequent soul-*
5   *searching she subjects herself to. The monolog contains some*
6   *very fast transitions between Mira's thoughts and emotions,*
7   *and the actor must discover these ideas and emotional states*
8   *moment-by-moment. Also challenging is the monolog's final*
9   *section which should be played as the exciting, outward-*
10   *directed climax to the piece — not as an introverted,*
11   *agonizing, soul-searching moment.*
12

13   **Listen, I got the job! They called me two hours ago! I**
14   **still can't believe it. You should have seen the**
15   **competition. They're getting younger every year. I was**
16   **talking to this one. I swear she looked like a high school**
17   **freshman. Perfect. Beautiful. She said she was twenty-**
18   **two. I looked around the room and they all looked —**
19   **fourteen! When I got out of there I felt — you know —**
20   **that I needed to examine myself. I went to the subway,**
21   **I went down to the platform and looked a long time in**
22   **the gum mirror. And I said to myself, you will be thirty**
23   **in six months. And you know — I can see it! For the first**
24   **time I can see lines under my eyes and around my**
25   **mouth. How long do you suppose they've been there?**
26   **The point is I recognize something about myself. I can't**
27   **tell you how beautiful the skin on that young girl was.**
28   **Her cheeks were as soft and smooth as gardenia petals.**
29   **Death itself couldn't have startled me so much. You**

1   know what I'm talking about, don't you? It scares me
2   because I didn't see it coming. It makes me wonder
3   about the inside of me. Am I less flexible in my thinking?
4   Do I feel as much as I did? Is it real what I feel? Will I
5   learn more as I grow older, or does the mind shrink with
6   the skin?
7
8
9
10
11
12
13
14
15
16
17
18
19
20
21
22
23
24
25
26
27
28
29
30
31
32
33
34
35

Sea of Forms
by Megan Terry

1   Two – 20s   Male or Female – Seriocomic

2

3   *This monolog gives the actor a built-in vis-à-vis for strong*
4   *communication, and an exciting situation for the actor to*
5   *play. The excitement, though, shouldn't be played as a news*
6   *flash — energy should also spring from Two's enthusiasm for*
7   *the discovery that he/she is announcing. Above all, the*
8   *tender moments and humorous references should be inserted*
9   *deftly, like soft counterpoint, to the overall pace and intensity*
10   *of the main narrative.*

11

12   **Have you heard: that the latest headline from the**
13   **biology lab is a fact of exquisite beauty? Did you know**
14   **that if you allow a scientist to extract two, only two, two**
15   **out of the billions of cells in your body, to pluck these**
16   **two cells from you and place them side-by-side in a**
17   **Pyrex dish — that these two cells without a philharmonic**
18   **orchestra — that these two cells — without a conductor**
19   **— that these two cells — without the shelter of you —**
20   **that these two cells, on their own in the wide world, will**
21   **beat together in a perfect pulse. Will pulse together in a**
22   **perfect beat. As long as they are together, outside of**
23   **you on the Pyrex dish, they will beat as lovers' hearts**
24   **beat. Two together, in harmony as one. But — if you**
25   **separate these cells, and place one cell in one of your**
26   **grandmother's Pyrex dishes and the other in another**
27   **dish, they will beat separately. The same two cells from**
28   **the same body, they will beat on their own and alone.**

29

The Web
by Martha Boesing

1 Abigail — 28   Female — Comic

2

3 *This ladder-type monolog is built on a comic contrast*

4 *between a normally conservative teacher and her sexual*

5 *metaphors that eventually emerge and take over as she*

6 *"lectures:" Abigail becomes increasingly carried away by her*

7 *fantasies as the speech develops. One of the peculiar*

8 *challenges here, however, is to avoid simplifying Abigail,*

9 *reducing her to some sort of feminist caricature. She makes*

10 *some valid points, and the actor should try to sustain the*

11 *tension between an informed, scholarly presentation and a*

12 *whacked-out declaration of gender politics.*

13

14 **The interesting thing about Aristotle's theory of tragedy**

15 **is its kinship to the male orgasm. You know, I have to**

16 **tell you how pleased I am that so many of you signed up**

17 **for this course. It means a great deal to me. It's so ...**

18 **unexpected ... Consider the standard that the first four**

19 **acts of a good play be built to a slow crescendo, rising**

20 **up and up, at an ever-increasing intensity of emotion,**

21 **until finally the climax is reached and there is a**

22 **tremendous outburst of passion, a catharsis, if you will,**

23 **after which, in the fifth act, a speedy decrescendo**

24 **immersing the hero in an overwhelming sense of**

25 **exhaustion, expenditure and loss, until he comes to his**

26 **final resting place, usually in death. Given this classical**

27 **format of biological determinism it follows that women's**

28 **plays could or should be multiorgasmic in form, small**

29 **mini-scenes perhaps, coming in waves of emotions,**

1   crests and valleys, like the ebb and flow of changing
2   tides, and finally consummating in a sense of
3   nourishment and plenitude, the creation of new life,
4   birth.
5
6
7
8
9
10
11
12
13
14
15
16
17
18
19
20
21
22
23
24
25
26
27
28
29
30
31
32
33
34
35

Night Luster

by Laura Harrington

Roma — 20s | Female — Serious

This ladder-type monolog contains a wonderful palette of emotional colors. The vis-à-vis is probably best played as a confidante; and there are two challenges here. One is to identify the three or four needs Roma is describing, and then give them a pattern or shape in performance that can be played effectively from beginning to the final climax. The other challenge is to avoid allowing the "dream" section to defuse the energy or slow the pace of the monolog. Roma's description of her dream should not be played as a nostalgic, winsome moment of indulgence, but instead as a puzzling non sequitur of which she's struggling to make sense.

I don't know. I get this feeling sometimes like I'm invisible or something. I can be standing there in a room and I'm talking and everything, and it's like my words aren't getting anywhere and I look down at myself and *Jesus!* Sometimes my body isn't getting anywhere either. It's like I'm standing behind a one-way mirror and I can see the guys and I can hear the guys but they can't see me and they can't hear me. And I start to wonder if maybe I'm ugly or something, like maybe I'm some alien species from another planet, and I don't speak the language and I look totally weird. But I don't know this, you see, because on this other planet I had this really nice mother who told me I was beautiful and that I had a voice to die for because she loved me so much, not because it was true. And I arrive here on

1 earth and I'm so filled with her love and her belief in me
2 that I walk around like I'm beautiful and I sing like I have
3 a voice to die for. And because I'm so convinced and so
4 strange and so *deluded,* people *pretend* to listen to me...
5 because they're being polite or something — or maybe
6 they're afraid of me. And at first I don't notice because
7 I sing with my eyes closed. But then one day I open my
8 eyes and I find out I'm living in this world where nobody
9 sees me and nobody hears me. I'm just lookin' for that
10 one guy who's gonna hear me, see me, ...really take a
11 chance. I mean, I *hear* them. I'm listening so hard, I hear
12 promises when somebody's just sayin' hello. Jesus, if
13 anybody ever heard what I've got locked up inside of me,
14 I'd be a *star.*
15
16
17
18
19
20
21
22
23
24
25
26
27
28
29
30
31
32
33
34
35

When the Bough Breaks
by Robert Clyman

1   Mary — 20s   Female — Comic
2
3   *Mary is a peppy, upbeat and optimistic nurse working a*
4   *maternity ward. She's sappy and sentimental, and also*
5   *totally devoted to her whacko husband, a defrocked Jesuit*
6   *priest. Her unquestioning belief in his absurd opinions lies at*
7   *the root of comedy in this piece. The humor doesn't need to*
8   *be forced and Mary should be played with all sincerity.*
9   *Notice that the monolog's concluding remarks can probably*
10 *be effectively played either comically or seriously, which*
11 *gives the actor an interesting challenge.*
12
13 You're worrying about your little boy, aren't you? Three
14 months early like this. You find it hard to understand
15 why God chose you. He always does the right thing, you
16 know. Frank, my fiancé, every Saturday night he and
17 God get into these rousing arguments. Frank says if
18 God didn't want us to ... you know ... He wouldn't have
19 built disreputable motels. Frank used to be a Jesuit, so
20 I figure he knows what he's talking about. He says God
21 was pretty wild Himself when He was young, so even
22 though He has infinite wisdom when it comes to things
23 like giving alms to the poor, He's like a reformed smoker
24 when it comes to sex. God loves each of us, but He has
25 a special place in His heart for preemies. Why, His own
26 son was a preemie. Frank says He sent His son to be
27 with us before we were ready. But if God had waited, we
28 wouldn't have had to wait to learn what perfection is.
29 Frank thinks that preemies are God's way of teaching

1   us about perfection. Because there's nothing else alive
2   that's so vulnerable. And we're never closer to
3   perfection than when we're loving something vulnerable.
4   There's no grace in loving something strong.
5
6
7
8
9
10
11
12
13
14
15
16
17
18
19
20
21
22
23
24
25
26
27
28
29
30
31
32
33
34
35

Stuck
by Adele Edling Shank

1 Margaret — 23	Female — Seriocomic

2

3   *This highly unusual speech permits the actress to play strong*
4   *anger towards her vis-à-vis, and then to turn the monolog*
5   *directly at the auditors. It's both a rejection of her lover and*
6   *a declaration of her personal rights. Though it may at times*
7   *sound like a speech on women's rights, the actress should*
8   *avoid a strident manner — her real confidante or vis-a-vis is*
9   *the audience! This challenging selection also permits several*
10   *different interpretations.*

11

12   **You stop that! Don't you ever talk to me that way again!**
13   **I've tried to be patient and be nice, but I'm sick and**
14   **tired of your talking as if you're the only person in the**
15   **world. You're a great big grown-up man and you asked**
16   **me to have an affair with you, remember? I was as nice**
17   **to you as I could be for as long as I could be, and if that**
18   **wasn't good enough then it's your fault, not mine.** *(To the*
19   *audience)* **I'm tired of being the bad guy. Oh, you don't**
20   **say anything, but I know you all think I treated him**
21   **mean. But you don't understand! It wasn't easy. I tried**
22   **for months, oh God! For months, to shake loose. But he**
23   **cried, and he sniveled. Oh, I got so fed up! But I didn't**
24   **let on. I mean I think he's kind of — delicate, and I really**
25   **didn't want to hurt him more than I had to, but I mean**
26   **really, a woman can only do so much! I did. I tried. But**
27   **he was never happy, you know that? When he was with**
28   **me he was always moaning about his wife. And I'll just**
29   **bet you when he was with her he was moaning about**

1   me. I mean, what did he think it was going to be
2   anyway, this affair he asked me to have, all Hollywood
3   moonlight and no guilt? When I find a man I think is
4   good for me I go and get him and when I think he isn't
5   good for me anymore, it's over. And what's wrong with
6   that?
7
8
9
10
11
12
13
14
15
16
17
18
19
20
21
22
23
24
25
26
27
28
29
30
31
32
33
34
35

Abingdon Square
by Maria Irene Fornés

1 Marion — 24	Female — Serious

2

3   *The actor should read this piece carefully in order to uncover*
4   *the many desperate emotions Marion experiences as she*
5   *speaks. The monolog presents a strong challenge to the actor*
6   *to fully play each painful turn of thought, each terrible*
7   *discovery, each difficult decision that Marion makes. She has*
8   *just left her husband for another man, and her frustration at*
9   *being separated from her child now compels her to question*
10   *this new relationship, and question herself most of all.*

11

12   **I need my child. I need my child, Minnie. I need that**
13   **child in my arms and I don't see a way I could ever have**
14   **him again. He has been irrevocably taken from me.**
15   **There is nothing I could do that would bring him back to**
16   **me. I have begged him to let me see him. I have gone**
17   **on my knees, I have offered myself to him. I have offered**
18   **my life to him. He won't listen. He won't forgive me. I'm**
19   **at his mercy. I wish for his death. I stalk the house. I**
20   **stand on the corner and I watch the house. I imagine the**
21   **child inside playing in his room. When spring comes I**
22   **may be able to see him in the garden. I know he's not**
23   **there, but that's how I can feel him near me. Looking at**
24   **the house. He's gone mad! He's insane, Minnie. Yes!**
25   **He's insane! He wants to destroy me. But I'll destroy**
26   **him first.**

27

28

29

Wetter Than Water
by Deborah Pryor

1   Chantel — 18   Female — Comic

2

3   *Chantel is describing for her vis-a-vis her godforsaken little*

4   *island in southern Louisiana. More than amusing, though,*

5   *Chantel is also a bit whacko, and this permits the actor to*

6   *introduce some very interesting character traits into the*

7   *interpretation. Finally, Chantel is also a fox, who enjoys*

8   *"putting on" the newcomer and trying to impress him.*

9

10   So I'm gonna teach you all about the native ways? Turn

11   you from a tourist into a local in three easy steps?

12   Some very important rules. One. You may have noticed

13   the sun. It's bad news. Maybe not other places, but

14   here it's so bright it shows you everything. And you

15   don't want to be seeing everything. So get some extra

16   dark glasses. Two. Gotta keep a monster gun by your

17   bed at night. Gotta shoot 'em on sight and show 'em

18   who's boss right away. I'm serious, Jack. Three. Stick

19   to the road. 'Cause of all the heat and the color, you're

20   liable to see things that ain't there and get all off your

21   course. Things falling apart and breaking down in the

22   tall grass. Big flowers rearing at you, poking you in the

23   collarbone. Possums hanging upside down make faces

24   at you, trying to get you to look at them. Don't —

25   whatever you do. Dark glasses, monster ammo, take

26   the straight and narrow. Simple as that. We keep

27   scorpions for pets — this big! Sometimes, I'm lying

28   awake in the dark and I can hear them along the floor.

29   They keep armadillos for pets. They have dances and

1   **it sounds like championship bowling on TV. Gotcha!**
2   **Better run for help now, mister!**
3
4
5
6
7
8
9
10
11
12
13
14
15
16
17
18
19
20
21
22
23
24
25
26
27
28
29
30
31
32
33
34
35

The Old Settler
by John Henry Redwood

1   Lou Bessie — 28   African-American Female — seriocomic

2

3   *Bessie is a young "woman about town" in WWII Harlem and*
4   *her former boyfriend, Husband, has come to New York to seek*
5   *her out and marry her. Here she's arguing with two older*
6   *women, friends of Husband, who are trying to keep Lou*
7   *Bessie away from him. They feel that Bessie will just*
8   *manipulate him with her city ways and run off after she's*
9   *used up his money. The piece has several important climaxes*
10   *which must be carefully structured by the actress, and also a*
11   *few revealing moments about Lou Bessie's true nature which*
12   *make her more than just the stereotype of a big city hustler.*

13

14   I can't wait long. Tonight's "Kitchen Mechanics Night"
15   at the Savoy Ballroom. I know Husband can't wait to
16   see me. He's nuts about me. He used to follow me all
17   over down home. Got on my nerves so bad sometimes!
18   Kept after me to marry him. I wasn't going to marry
19   nobody and get stuck down there in Frogmore ... and
20   him tied to his mama like he was ... Uh, uh, not me. I'm
21   so glad to be up here in Harlem. I used to hear about
22   Harlem all the time when I was a little girl and I knew
23   when I was fourteen that as soon as I could, I was
24   coming to Harlem! I ain't never seen so many colored
25   people in one place in all my life. Parties, dances, shows,
26   jazz, parades and music going on all the time ... Even
27   preachers standing on ladders in the streets, preaching.
28   And now Harlem is full of all those fine-looking colored
29   soldiers from Fort Dix. No siree, I wasn't going to marry

1   nobody and miss this ... Yeah, well, maybe now that he
2   ain't tied to his mama things might be different between
3   him and me. We can maybe get us a place on Sugar Hill
4   or even Striver's Row. Paul Robeson lives on Striver's
5   Row, you know. Then if Husband goes into the army,
6   they will send some of his money home as an allotment
7   ... He ain't got to worry. They ain't going to let no colored
8   soldiers fight in the war. That's what's so good about it.
9   He can go in the army and they will pay him and give him
10   one of those pretty uniforms and he ain't got to worry
11   about getting killed. Now, with the allotment and
12   whatever money he has from his mama, we can open up
13   a combination beauty salon/barber shop ... maybe right
14   across the street from the Savoy Ballroom where there's
15   a lot of traffic.
16
17
18
19
20
21
22
23
24
25
26
27
28
29
30
31
32
33
34
35

Truth: The Testimonial of Sojourner Truth
adapted by Eric Coble

1 Sojourner Truth — Teens   African-American Female — Serious
2
3 *Sojourner Truth was a famous human rights activist of the*
4 *mid-nineteenth century. Here she recalls her childhood as a*
5 *young slave girl, describing some of her living conditions and*
6 *personal fears, and even "acting out" some of the*
7 *punishments she received from her white masters. As the*
8 *piece develops, the young girl begins to speak more and more*
9 *"directly" to God, invoking His protection. The monolog is*
10 *extremely challenging because it must be presented with the*
11 *childlike naiveté of a very young, uneducated girl,*
12 *improvising and pretending the simulated voices of other*
13 *characters, yet still achieve a maximum of belief and*
14 *sincerity. The actor must not approach it technically, but*
15 *emotionally and spiritually.*
16
17 Down in the cellar. Mud and puddles. Mens and womens
18 sleepin' all in the same big lump. Tiny little old window
19 and a little stick of firewood, and Mau-Mau talkin' 'bout
20 things — 'bout my eleven, twelve brothers and sisters
21 sold away, taken off, but not me. I'm stayin' forever.
22 'Cause I'm the littlest. And pappy's name is Bomfree
23 and that means "tall tree" and tall trees protect little
24 girls and if he doesn't 'cause he's old and more like a
25 "bent tree," then God will, right, Mau-Mau, right? But
26 where does God live? "In the sky, child. You see them
27 stars and clouds and moon? God made all of 'em. And
28 when you fall into any trouble, you ask Him for help. Ask
29 Him and He'll hear you and He'll help you. Anyone can

43

1   make a moon can help a little girl." And I wondered if
2   You heard her when they took my brothers away. But she
3   say, "Isabella, this very same moon and these very same
4   stars you're lookin' at are lookin' back down over your
5   brothers and sisters, just as they're lookin' up to see
6   them. God, He knows where we all are." But He's the
7   only one. 'Cause the very same stars and moon looked
8   down when I was sold to Master Nealy. Mau-Mau Bett
9   and Bomfree were sold off to die in some cellar, blind
10   and freezing. Mau-Mau didn't even die where God could
11   see her — *(SHE tumbles across the stage as if shoved.)* ...
12   Yes, Master Nealy, I know — the pot hooks — I thought
13   you say frying pan — your English is too fast, all I got is
14   my Dutch, but Master, the Mistress says not on a
15   Sunday ... not on Sunday ... not ... *(SHE spins around as*
16   *though whipped.)* ... on ... Sunday...*(Again and again, SHE*
17   *sinks lower with every blow, until SHE is a crumpled mass*
18   *on the floor. Pause.)* I can still feel the blood running wet
19   down my ankles. But I do it. I remember Mau-Mau's
20   words — I pray and I'm grittin' my teeth and I'm prayin'
21   — and God answers me. Every time. Only problem is
22   when I get beat I never see it comin' enough ahead of
23   time to pray. And there's the trick. See, I know You can't
24   hear anythin' 'cept what's spoke out loud. That's why I
25   made our little clearing in the mud of the river — nothing
26   here but the wind through the branches and water
27   washing grains of sand. Here I can tell what I need to tell
28   and You hear me, right? Can't expect You to read minds,
29   now can I? But I don't like bein' overheard by nobody.
30   We're private.
31
32
33
34
35

Nightfall With Edgar Allan Poe
by Eric Coble

1   Helen Whitman — 20s   Female — Serious

2

3   *Helen is Poe's ex-fiancée trying to prevent a surgeon from*

4   *cutting open Poe's body in autopsy. The piece offers the actor*

5   *a wonderful opportunity to create a gripping, spooky mood*

6   *from the outset with a fascinating challenge to the actor's use*

7   *of voice and powers of imagination. Of particular interest here*

8   *is the pattern of pauses the actor chooses to establish as*

9   *Helen focuses William's attention on the corpse of Edgar Allan*

10   *Poe which lies before them.*

11

12   **Shhh. William. Shhh. Shhh. I want you to do something**

13   **with me. Will you help me? Look at me. Please look at**

14   **me. You don't just want facts, do you? You want**

15   **secrets. Don't you. Look at Edgar. Just watch him. His**

16   **corpse ... or more precisely ... look at the air just over**

17   **the corpse. Keep your gaze on the space just above his**

18   **body — so that he exists only in your peripheral vision.**

19   **Don't move. Just watch. And listen. I can feel your**

20   **pulse. Through your skin. Can you feel mine? I saw him**

21   **move. When we were talking earlier, I was staring at**

22   **him, at his body ... and I saw it move. You're trembling.**

23   **Keep watching. He'll move again. Not directly, not**

24   **empirically ... but out of the corner of your eye, you'll**

25   **see it. Keep watching the air above him. If you look**

26   **straight on at him, he'll be dead. Just a corpse. But**

27   **that's not what's real, William. Truth is what you catch**

28   **in your peripheral vision. By the time you see something**

29   **head-on, it's had a chance to collect itself. To twist**

1   what's real into what's expected. The real Edgar Allan
2   Poe was never who he appeared to be either ... You can't
3   look straight on ...
4
5
6
7
8
9
10
11
12
13
14
15
16
17
18
19
20
21
22
23
24
25
26
27
28
29
30
31
32
33
34
35

Sally's Gone, She Left Her Name
by Russell Davis

1 Sally — 17   Female — Serious
2
3 *This monolog contains strong emotional colors right from the*
4 *outset, and permits the actor a clear vis-à-vis. Christopher is*
5 *Sally's brother and she desperately needs his understanding*
6 *because their mother has left the home and Sally feels at*
7 *fault. Though her confusion is evident, she clearly develops*
8 *more confidence by the time she finishes. There is also a*
9 *strong challenge here to avoid playing Sally as too defeated*
10 *and beaten down by her situation. This is the speech of a*
11 *person trying to win understanding — not to whine about her*
12 *condition.*
13
14 Chris, everyone says corny stuff in private. In particular,
15 me. I say things in my head, hopes, stuff like that, that
16 sound just awful when I say them out loud. I've tried it.
17 Doesn't sound at all like it did when I just thought it.
18 It's the same with everybody. The same, I bet. 'Cause
19 there's some kind of background music inside your
20 head. If I say in my head, for example, I love you,
21 Christopher, there's a background music. Otherwise
22 how could I say it? I don't mean there's music, Chris,
23 but something, and I can get goosebumps on my arms
24 from thinking about you, Christopher. I can. But if I
25 actually said to you, I love you, Christopher, immediately
26 I would feel phony or something's awkward. And we'd
27 have to argue right away to get back to normal. And I
28 don't understand how come. How come you have to
29 keep it in your head. How come the older you get, the

1   more and more stuff you have to keep in your head. Any
2   kind of hopes you ever had about living, all of it inside
3   your head, until you can't hold it up anymore, and you're
4   ashamed, and you fall over, get old, and die. *(Pause.)* I
5   love you, Christopher. *(Pause.)* I love dad, too. *(Pause.)*
6   Mom. *(Pause.)* I love you, mom, from as far away as you
7   have to get from me.
8
9
10
11
12
13
14
15
16
17
18
19
20
21
22
23
24
25
26
27
28
29
30
31
32
33
34
35

Night Train To Bolina
by Nilo Cruz

1	Sister Nora — 30s
2	

1   Sister Nora — 30s   Female — Serious
2
3   *This monolog has two very clearly-defined vis-à-vis, two*
4   *orphan children at a Catholic orphanage somewhere in*
5   *Central America. It also offers the added challenge of*
6   *beginning. in a somewhat "quiet" mood, and gradually*
7   *changing into a brisk and efficient delivery style. Although it*
8   *may seem nostalgic and depressing, it can effectively be*
9   *played as a development from thoughtfulness to optimism*
10   *and confidence. In the original play, young Clara sits on a*
11   *chair in the center of the stage, Sister Nora stands behind her*
12   *braiding her hair, and Clara is braiding Talita's hair, who is*
13   *kneeling in front of her.*
14
15   There used to be a time when the needs of this place
16   were fulfilled, and children like you spent the whole day
17   in classrooms, learning how to read and write. Now
18   there's not enough of us and this place is falling apart.
19   Everything smells of mold. As when things become
20   moldy and moth eaten. There used to be a time when
21   this building was airy and sanitary, because we had time
22   to scrub our walls and floors. We had time to maintain
23   our gardens, to cut down the branches from our trees
24   and let in the fresh air. And in the summertime we used
25   to throw buckets of water on the floor, flooding the
26   mission up to our ankles, so the tiles could retain the
27   cool moist and soothe the heat. Our walls were painted
28   and there were no leaks on our roofs. Then things
29   changed. No missionaries wanted to come here to work.

1   And others left frightened of danger. Afraid of getting
2   killed or lost in our jungles, to end up mangled or
3   mutilated by guerrillas or soldiers. So now if the alms
4   box needs to be painted, we take a brush and paint it.
5   All you children have to help us. If there's no one to
6   mend the altar cloths, we take a needle and thread and
7   mend them. You know how to sweep and dust, Clara?
8   Good. You can sweep and dust the parish. Take a broom
9   and duster from the room next to the vestry. Talita, you
10   take her there and show her where they're kept. Show
11   her how to sweep under the prayer stools. To get
12   underneath the stools with the broom. Dirt accumulates
13   down there. And show her how to polish the pulpit and
14   the altar rails. The altar cloths are washed on Mondays.
15   The candles are also changed on that day. I like to
16   change them on Mondays, because Mondays are dull and
17   somber. New candles brighten up the church and bring
18   clarity. When you clean the saints use soap and water.
19   Not too much soap or you'll get too much foam. Then it
20   will take you forever to rinse them. Make sure you dry
21   them well with the cloth I set aside for them. Talita will
22   show you. You know, that's one thing I always liked
23   doing, washing the saints and angels. I like to bathe
24   them as if they were my children. Clean their ears and
25   elbows real good, as I would do a baby. And talk to
26   them. They like it when you talk to them. They like to
27   listen.
28
29
30
31
32
33
34
35

This One Thing I Do
by Claire Braz-Valentine

1 Susan B. Anthony — 20s   Female — Serious
2
3 *This impassioned speech gives the actor an opportunity to*
4 *use her language skills, to express many deeply-felt emotions,*
5 *and to create a strong relationship with her vis-à-vis. As is*
6 *usual with formal speeches, the actor should avoid the*
7 *temptation to fall into a declamatory style that is uni-*
8 *dimensional and that limits the emotional palette to little*
9 *more than a harangue.*
10
11 I will not tolerate this any longer. To learn what? To
12 listen to what? Drivel about how all male teachers are
13 paid so little when every woman in this room is a
14 teacher and every one of them earns only a fifth of what
15 you men earn? How can any of you be so foolish as to
16 sit and wonder why your salaries are so low? Look
17 behind you, gentlemen. Your answer is sitting there in
18 enforced silence. What do you expect? Teaching is the
19 only profession that is not closed to women. Society
20 demands that women be kept poor. Cannot be self-
21 sufficient. And even at one-fifth of what you make,
22 they're not going to raise the teachers' salaries, because
23 if they raise yours, then they raise ours, and women
24 must be kept at the poverty level. All of you sitting here
25 and bemoaning the fact that you make so little, and we
26 here with the same duties, some of us with more
27 responsibility, make so much less. So you see, if you
28 want to raise your salaries, you're going to have to focus
29 yourselves on a more important issue, that of equal pay

1   for all people. This can be the first milestone in equal pay
2   for women. Demand that women's salaries be equal.
3
4
5
6
7
8
9
10
11
12
13
14
15
16
17
18
19
20
21
22
23
24
25
26
27
28
29
30
31
32
33
34
35

Blue Skies Forever
by Claire Braz-Valentine

1   Amelia — 30s   Female — Serious
2
3   *This challenging piece is a stepping-stone type of monolog,*
4   *where the actor grapples with one point after another as she*
5   *attempts to explain to later generations who she is and why*
6   *she undertook to achieve what no woman before her had ever*
7   *attempted. The actor must observe the playwright's*
8   *suggestions for structuring the piece according to a clearly*
9   *defined pattern of "beats" as she moves through the*
10   *performance, in order for the presentation to develop and*
11   *provide an overall "shape" to Amelia Earhart's thoughts. This*
12   *monolog is written to be Amelia's response to all the*
13   *speculation about her mysterious life and disappearance.*
14   *Amelia Earhart enters. She is in full flight regalia: brown*
15   *leather jacket, jodhpurs, boots, long scarf and flight helmet.*
16
17   When I'm in the air, away from ... this earth, when I'm
18   not land-bound, it's like I've gone through a window ...
19   a portal of reality, and then out the other side ... and I'm
20   floating along the seam of the universe, and I am free in
21   the solitude of centuries. And no one knows my name,
22   my gender. When I am in that space between heaven
23   and earth, where so few women have been, people don't
24   know what to make of me. They call me a loner. They
25   say I'm different, difficult to understand, cool, aloof,
26   withdrawn, preoccupied. Of course they are right. I'm
27   worse than that. I am a dangerous woman. I am a
28   determined woman. I am not normal. I live for life at the
29   edge ... where nothing stagnates, nothing's the same. I

1   walk that high wire into the great adventure. And I love
2   every minute of it. This is what I've always wanted. And
3   I have no patience waiting for the times to change to
4   catch up with me. They will never catch up. *(Beat.)* When
5   I am in the air ... I am where I belong ... in that place
6   where nothing stands still, everything moves, and it's
7   never boring. Everything is always new. It's always the
8   first time in the theater of angels, of birds ... the
9   kingdom of wings. My body feels heavy on land. My
10 bones are solid. *(Beat.)* When I am up there soaring...
11 through the fingers of God, with my hand on the throttle,
12 I am beyond woman or man, above gender, and the lust
13 of earthly sex, the longings of simple skin. When I am up
14 there in the beautiful blindness of clouds, I am above it
15 all ... of having to fit in, of being accepted and desired,
16 of being what's expected. I am the unexpected, the
17 unforeseen. I am your astonishment. I am on the other
18 side. Where no one judges you by the shape of your
19 body, the length of your hair, the color of your skin, the
20 lines on your face, or the cut of your clothes. I am
21 released. Free. *(Beat.)* I don't want to land. I want more
22 space. I don't want to land. *(Beat.)* I always expected
23 everything, and I ignored the rules, the rules against
24 women. The roles against women. I was not born to
25 follow rules or to play a role, for anyone. I was born to
26 search, to push, to try something new, to let other
27 women know they must not be caged. To give them
28 freedom. To tell them they are not playthings, but
29 players. It's all there for them. The only price they pay to
30 get it is courage. Once you have courage the doors are
31 open. And you go through them. And once you go
32 through these doors, you are in the company of daring
33 women, dangerous women, dear women who will inspire
34 you, challenge you, lead you to the horizons of your
35 dreams. *(Beat.)* Honor knows no gender. Courage knows

1   no gender. *(Beat.)* I have stood before hundreds of
2   thousands and said these words and it was written that
3   I wore a blue dress with matching necklace, that I was
4   gracious, almost lovely, thoroughly feminine, not like a
5   boy at all. I have flown beside my courageous sisters
6   who have crashed and died in the pursuit of their
7   independence and their dreams, and it is called a
8   Powder Puff Derby, the Sweethearts of the Air. We are
9   not America's sweethearts. And, no, we are not like
10   boys at all. *(Beat.)*
11   I have paid my dues to become this woman.
12   I married my promoter who raised the money to pay
13   for my plane.
14   I will use it to leave him.
15   I will use it to leave everyone,
16   Even myself.
17   I did not love him nor his earthbound sex,
18   But I would have spread my legs for the devil
19   So I could spread my wings.
20   *(Beat.)*
21   They call my plane Electra,
22   Electra who longed for her father.
23   I long for no man ... I long for air.
24   I yearn for freedom at any price.
25   At the ultimate price.
26   I lift
27   I thrust
28   I pitch I roll
29   I spin
30   I glide above you
31   I am
32   Airborne
33   Out of your reach
34   Away from your eyes
35   Closer to God.

1	Forever.
2	The sky is my lover, my destiny.
3	They call me Lady Lindy,
4	But I am no lady.
5	My name is Amelia,
6	And I am
7	A Flier.
8	*(SHE raises her arms until they are outstretched. SHE is*
9	*smiling.)*
10	
11	
12	
13	
14	
15	
16	
17	
18	
19	
20	
21	
22	
23	
24	
25	
26	
27	
28	
29	
30	
31	
32	
33	
34	
35	

Punk Girls
by Elizabeth Wong

1 Green Punk — 20s   Asian-American Female—Seriocomic
2
3 *This monolog is taken from a short ten-minute play about*
4 *two Generation X-ers, both young Asian-American teens, who*
5 *get ready for a "rave" (tr.: party) by spray-painting their hair,*
6 *and talking seriously about theological matters of good and*
7 *evil. They want to know what they can do, if anything, to*
8 *make the world a better place. This play is also an insider's*
9 *joke, an homage to the playwright Tony Kushner, and it was*
10 *commissioned by Megan Terry and the Omaha Magic Theatre*
11 *for inclusion in a larger work called "EXPLOR-A-TORI-YUM,"*
12 *funded by the Rockefeller Foundation. Green Punk is dressed*
13 *in "dangerous" clothing. She has a spray paint can in her*
14 *hand.*
15
16 **How can you be so calm? I'm in a crisis here! This is**
17 **eating me up from the inside-out! I'm stinking. And**
18 **putrid from the rot of my own pathetic spiritual**
19 **indifference. Explain it to me. Help me to understand.**
20 **I'm lost. The universe is exploding. It's blowing up. It's**
21 **·a car bomb right in our very souls** (*GREEN PUNK paints*
22 *"NO HOPE" on the wall or floor.*) **I'm bubbling, gurgling in**
23 **a death grip ... and you talk about the goodness of the**
24 **universe? The goodness of God? I'm talking about**
25 **human suffering. I'm talking about the enormous**
26 **amount of human pain arising from omnipotent design.**
27 **Poverty, oppression, persecution, war, injustice,**
28 **indignity, inequity. These are evils, manifestations of**
29 **sin. Palpable, inescapable, undeniable. This is the**

1   dilemma of our age. This is the question. This is the root
2   cause of helplessness, and hopelessness, and universal
3   despondency, and rap music! Stop the Bahranians from
4   clitorectomies. Stop children from toiling for slave
5   wages. Restore the Dalai Lama! Save Sri Lanka from
6   genocide. Save Kosovo from genocide. Mass graves in
7   Rwanda. Mass graves in Bosnia. Mass graves in
8   Cambodia. The starving in Korea. The starving
9   everywhere. Decaying families under secret graves. The
10   hand of God, the artwork of God in man. One million
11   dead in Rwanda. Two million refugees in Tanzania. And
12   Burundi. Oh God, what about Burundi? Poor little
13   Burundi. Where is Burundi? Where is God? And you
14   wonder why G.H.B., Xtasy!! And the rain forest!
15   Unspeakable acts of suffering by governments, by
16   military minds, warring tribes, political factionalism!
17   Tears of innocent war-torn children! Soaking the crust of
18   the earth, right down to the grave ... crystal, pot, speed,
19   Drano, laughing gas? Let's pray. *(Softly, muttering)*
20   Microsoft, Merck, R.J. Reynolds, I.B.M., Microsoft,
21   Sony, Hallmark, Microsoft, Proctor, Gamble, Microsoft.
22   *(GREEN PUNK falls to her knees, mumbling a fervent prayer.)*
23
24
25
26
27
28
29
30
31
32
33
34
35

Cleveland Raining
by Sung Rno

1	Mari — 20s	Asian-American Female — Serious

2

3   *Mari and her brother have been abandoned by their parents*
4   *and have been living in the family's modest home in rural*
5   *Ohio for some time. In fact, Mari's father just drove off rather*
6   *recently and she's been trying to locate him by driving*
7   *obsessively around the state in hopes of finding some trace of*
8   *his whereabouts. In the play, she's speaking here to her*
9   *friend who's sleeping; but by itself as a monolog performance*
10   *the actor can use the audience as a listener. Both Mari and*
11   *her brother have recurring bad dreams about their*
12   *abandonment, and here she begins by describing the content*
13   *of hers.*

14

15   *(Reading while writing)* **Someone's sticking their face**
16   **into the crib. I'm sleeping. I feel someone's lips. Soft.**
17   **Warm. There's that smell that I remember but I don't**
18   **know from where. I open my eyes, my baby eyes and I**
19   **see my brother's face. He looks sad, he looks scared.**
20   **Why are you scared, Oppah? Someone' shouting in the**
21   **other room. Someone's crying. I'm crying.** *(She stops*
22   *writing.)* **If that someone is me, then who is the other**
23   **someone? Can you tell me? A simple sign would do. I've**
24   **been driving for over a week now. Still no sign of him.**
25   **Driving so much my calluses have calluses. I dream in**
26   **interstate miles, in state highways that bump and jerk**
27   **through my head while I try to sleep. And still no sign.**
28   **Memory is my only weapon, my only hope. My friends**
29   **tell me to move on, to leave this place. They don't**

1 understand. Escape doesn't always solve things. You
2 can't just leave the places behind and expect everything
3 to be fine. The past finds you. What you've done before,
4 comes to your door today and tomorrow. Look at my
5 mother and father. They leave their country, Korea, they
6 come here, they make a better place. They think that
7 they can just pick up where they left off. Just lift the
8 needle off that record player, put another disc on, let the
9 needle drop back down again. But see, the music has
10 changed. You need different ears here. In this corn
11 country, this state where flat is a color, and gray is a
12 song. Are you getting all of this?
13
14
15
16
17
18
19
20
21
22
23
24
25
26
27
28
29
30
31
32
33
34
35

Night Breath
by Dennis Klontz

1   Two — 28   Female — Serious

2

3   *This thoughtful monolog has a strong narrative line in the*
4   *story of the miner. Although the tale does have a definite*
5   *beginning, middle and end, it doesn't readily offer the actor*
6   *any explosive high points. It's well suited to an actor who*
7   *can invest the narrative with special importance. One should*
8   *probably avoid the tendency to perform a quiet "memory*
9   *piece" that lacks energy, and instead play Two's puzzlement,*
10   *curiosity and search for meaning in the story as she's*
11   *speaking.*

12

13   **Rosie, she was staying in a temporary way, before**
14   **coming to California, in this small mining town out near**
15   **Ajo. Weren't much there. Just a bunch of copper miners**
16   **cussing Arizona with talk of Alaska and gold. Loud folk**
17   **they were. Big talking, big dreaming, small doing. All**
18   **pretty much alike. Excepting this one — fixing to go to**
19   **Alaska like the rest, but not for gold. Gonna get himself**
20   **a snow bear, a giant one with white fur all over. He ain't**
21   **never seen no white bear, so he figured it the most ...**
22   **special thing on God's created earth. Lord, how he**
23   **wanted that thing, that ... snow bear ... that miner. He**
24   **was all the time showing off this here steel trap he had**
25   **to catch the critter with. Rambling on and on 'bout that**
26   **snow bear like there was but one in the whole state of**
27   **Alaska. Specially drunk—whew! Would his tongue spark**
28   **fires! Well, one drunk night, God knows what he was**
29   **doing with that trap, but it snapped on him. Got him in**

1   the belly ... And ... ahh ... he's in our room, down on his
2   knees curled over that trap. Won't let nobody touch him.
3   Won't let them work the trap for fear his insides will fall
4   out if'n it opens up. And he gets strange, you know.
5   Confused 'bout things. Then, God knows how, that man
6   gets to his feet, holding on to that trap, and he carries it
7   with him out the door into the street. And damn if he's
8   not walking out of town thinking he's on his way to
9   Alaska ... Well, he makes it 'bout a quarter a mile before
10 collapsing. Rest of the night before dying. The whole
11 time thinking — believing — he's in Alaska. And ... ahh
12 ... right before the end he thinks he has trapped a snow
13 bear. Seems like everybody got their own kind of snow
14 bear they're after.
15
16
17
18
19
20
21
22
23
24
25
26
27
28
29
30
31
32
33
34
35

The Boiler Room
by Reuben Gonzalez

1   Olivia — 20s   Female — Serious

2

3   *This is a ladder-type of monolog which develops from a focus*

4   *on Olivia's concern for her mother to an even stronger focus*

5   *on Olivia's personal situation. It offers rich opportunities for*

6   *movement, and for a range of emotional colors: sadness,*

7   *hope, bitterness, frustration, love and encouragement, among*

8   *others. It's especially challenging because the actor must*

9   *sustain a clear dramatic build from start to finish.*

10

11   I had so many plans. Not just for me, Ma. For all of us.

12   Don't you think I wanted something better for you, too?

13   Don't you think that I wanted to get you out of here? You

14   don't know how many times I've driven past those big

15   fancy houses and swore that one day I was going to buy

16   one for you. I even know the one I'd buy you. It's right

17   on a corner in Stamford, with hedges and trees out

18   front. And in the back there's this area where they're

19   building a swimming pool. One day I even went around

20   the back of the house and watched as they cleared a

21   space for the pool. And you know what I wanted to do,

22   Ma? I wanted to say, "Hey, stop! Hey, my mother

23   doesn't want no swimming pool back there. She just

24   wants some dirt and some seeds so she can grow

25   things." Then I imagined you squatting back there

26   planting something just like in that picture with you and

27   Dona Lola in Puerto Rico. It's all so unfair, Ma.

28   Everything's so unfair. I listen to Anthony talking about

29   snatching pocketbooks and I look at him all dirty and

1   looking like he just come out of a war, and then I think
2   of all those other kids the same as Anthony without a
3   care in the world. The most they'll ever have to worry
4   about is first whether it will be Harvard or Yale, and then
5   later whether they will go into their daddy's business or
6   conquer some new turf of their own. It's all so unfair.
7   Those kids didn't have to work for that, Ma. One day
8   they were born and it was just there. They become
9   doctors, lawyers, politicians. They run for President.
10   They have their country clubs, their health clubs, their
11   country houses, their winter houses. They shop at
12   Bergdorff's and Bonwit's. They have lunch. They wear fur
13   coats. They have their faces made. I'll never be able to
14   do any of those things.
15
16
17
18
19
20
21
22
23
24
25
26
27
28
29
30
31
32
33
34
35

Interborough Transit
by Adam Kraar

1   Tanya — 20s   Female — Serious

2

3   *This interesting selection can be played in one of three ways:*

4   *as a naive comic presentation of pop clichés about parenting,*

5   *as the touching and serious hope of a very young woman*

6   *dreaming of her future family, or as a mixture of the two. In*

7   *either case, the actor must decide upon the degree of her own*

8   *personal belief in the character's thoughts, and her feeling*

9   *must be intense and sincere. The final moments of the piece*

10 *are also challenging, because the climax here takes the form*

11 *of a winsome hopefulness that cannot be played in a "flashy"*

12 *manner.*

13

14 **You want to hear my dream? My dream is simply to have**

15 **my own little girl. My own little girl. She'll have all my**

16 **potential, all my good looks, all my passion, all my sex,**

17 **but ... I'm gonna eat certain foods before I conceive her**

18 **so she'll never have a problem with weight. Of course I**

19 **won't drink or ... If you feed your child a certain way in**

20 **its first years, her temperament will be even. Spring**

21 **water, organic vegetables and no caffeine. And no**

22 **drugs, ever ... My plan is to raise her in an environment**

23 **where openness won't get her into trouble. Like a three**

24 **acre estate on the north shore. She won't have to go to**

25 **school if she doesn't want to; I'll tutor her at home ... I**

26 **see her as a dancer. She's going to invent a whole new**

27 **kind of dance where the dancers look like naked**

28 **children even with leotards on, and they move like cats**

29 **and gazelles and fawns. She'll have such an aura of**

1   innocence that no man will dare treat her bad ... You
2   know how some children can touch strangers and it's
3   not for any reason, just for the sake of touching, like
4   looking at a flower? No explanations, no hesitation, no
5   looking back. Now. Now. Now ... Anna will touch that
6   way.
7
8
9
10
11
12
13
14
15
16
17
18
19
20
21
22
23
24
25
26
27
28
29
30
31
32
33
34
35

Lady Liberty
by Adam Kraar

1   Ellen — 20s   Female — Seriocomic
2
3   *This monolog only seems to be a declaration of strength and*
4   *purpose. Actually, the actor must play it as a series of*
5   *discoveries for the character: Ellen is talking in order to*
6   *convince herself and figure out what to do with this man.*
7   *Certainly she needs her vis-à-vis to listen and reassure her,*
8   *but Ellen's real listener is herself. What is most unusual for*
9   *the actor here is the conclusion where Ellen at first seems*
10   *determined to hold on to Joey at all costs, but then briefly*
11   *"lowers her mask" to let us know she's not entirely*
12   *convinced that she's going to succeed when she speaks to*
13   *him that evening.*
14
15   Tonight is it. I'm layin' down the law. And if he doesn't
16   really want me the way I am — a meat eater, a
17   Springsteen lover and a drinker of fine American beers
18   — fine! I'm not gonna spend the rest of my life renting
19   a room from his dad. The worst thing in the world is to
20   be old and have nothing left but a plate fulla deep-fried
21   regrets. I want kids! I want a house, a rose garden and
22   a tomato farm in Bergen County. And if I live with a
23   man, I wanna know that it's for keeps. Especially with
24   Joey, who wakes up every morning with a new plan in
25   his head ... I'll tell you something else: he's never gonna
26   be happy with anyone except me. He thinks maybe he
27   could be, I see him looking, but he's in love with me. I
28   don't understand how people look for happiness
29   everywhere except right in front of their face. I can't talk

1	about it any more, I'm gonna bust a gut ... You think I'm
2	crazy? Don't answer ... I can't help it! He's part of me,
3	like my twisted little toe that always chafes, no matter
4	what shoes I wear ... Alright. Alright. If I have to, I can
5	walk without a little toe, right? ... Right.
6	
7	
8	
9	
10	
11	
12	
13	
14	
15	
16	
17	
18	
19	
20	
21	
22	
23	
24	
25	
26	
27	
28	
29	
30	
31	
32	
33	
34	
35	

Who Ever Said I Was a Good Girl?
by Gustavo Ott

1   Trixi — 15   Punk Female — Serious
2
3   *Trixi has killed thirty-one people, trying to maintain her status*
4   *among the gang members in a large city. In the play she*
5   *struggles to retain her hold on power, only to lose it in the*
6   *end. Here, she speaks to a new gang member, a girl of*
7   *thirteen who wants to be just like Trixi. Particularly*
8   *challenging is Trixi's speech pattern, broken and fragmented,*
9   *which she explains as follows: "It's that I can't ... It seems*
10   *like I just can't get the words to say ... when you feel or*
11   *you've gone through a thing ... I can't find words ... I don't*
12   *know ... to say things." Her words provide an important clue*
13   *to understanding her value system, and sympathizing with*
14   *her situation.*
15
16   **You don't know what I do. Then you better learn to do**
17   **what I do. It's the only way they'll think you're in charge.**
18   **In charge of your people and everyone else too. You**
19   **should learn to do what I do so they respect you ... you'll**
20   **be in ... with the people that get shit done. Living is ...**
21   **like if life was ... I mean ... I mean ... Living is shit. I**
22   **don't like living as much as ... I like other things better**
23   **than living ... Well, killing ... Living, for me it's ... that's**
24   **it. Killing. Let 'em show some respect when you're**
25   **sticking a serious piece in their face. That's living. The**
26   **rest is just fairy tales and TV. What was the first ... the**
27   **first time like? I remember it perfectly. She was my**
28   **grammar teacher. I was eleven. Young Lulu put a sweet**
29   **little .22 in my hands, it looked like a toy. I never**

1   thought I'd have one of those. I took it to school and if
2   anyone touched me, I stuck it in their chest. And that
3   day this teacher was sneering at me, she yelled at me in
4   front of the whole class. So I pulled out my .22 and shot
5   her right through the eye. Then I finished her off with one
6   in the gut. I learned two things. One: nobody talks to the
7   cops when they're scared. And two: no one ever
8   suspects eleven-year-old girls. And the rest? The same.
9   One after the other. Like in line. One day a bus driver,
10   then a taxi driver. Later on, some old guy. Orders from
11   Lulu, friends who need a favor, people who have things I
12   want, or people passing by when Quickdraw is catching
13   up with me. Total zeroes. People with no past or story.
14   Zombies. Like on TV. They die and there's nothing
15   behind them. I don't know their life anyway and that's
16   enough. They ... they ... they just show up asking to be
17   killed, like the woman in the drug store who wouldn't
18   give me an aspirin. I had a headache. You know? You
19   should understand. You know what's the best thing
20   you've done in your life? I'll tell you. The best thing
21   you've ever done in your life is talk to me. It is. And if
22   anything I've told you sticks in your head, you'll do all
23   right in this life.
24
25
26
27
28
29
30
31
32
33
34
35

A Tuesday in April
by Max Bush

1   Christina — 19   Female — Serious

2

3   *Christina is technically "schizo-affective" in the play, and in*

4   *the following monolog she's beginning a serious break with*

5   *reality. She speaks to a friend here, while drinking a heavy*

6   *dose of sleeping pills. However, the actor can ignore these*

7   *particularities of the actual play and invest this "mad scene"*

8   *with a number of personal associations or "substitutions"*

9   *from his or her own life. The piece also challenges the actor*

10   *to discover and play strong conflict. One should try to "play*

11   *the opposite" when performing this monolog: find what*

12   *Christina's struggling for, and avoid presenting Christine as*

13   *weak, defeated and sliding into passivity.*

14

15   **Is she gone?** *(Pause.)* **I hear the mountains in my ears.**

16   *(Pause.)* **When Leana was here my chromosomes started**

17   **breaking up. And they're on the floor, ready to crumble,**

18   **so I hid from her.** *(SHE turns to CRAIG, drinks.)* **You know**

19   **I used to know you. Your hair was white and your eyes**

20   **were green but you still loved me. Remember? I met you**

21   **in the Death Forest and the people were all too beautiful**

22   **to see, but they let me see them. But I couldn't touch**

23   **them. I wasn't ready. Then I had a baby and I got happy**

24   **for her. But they took her away and gave her to another**

25   **Father who hates her. So I'm helping her, too.** *(Pause.)* **I**

26   **loved you all my life and then I met you. In the Forest.**

27   **Remember? And you said "Growing up won't be hard. I**

28   **will love you. You'll know what I mean when you're**

29   **older." But my dad had two other daughters, and he**

1   loved them both, too, and divided up all the love and
2   gave it away from me. And when he touched me again I
3   was burned. But it was all my fault. I deserved it because
4   I didn't know how to love him, any more. Then he told
5   me that it wouldn't hurt growing up with people I didn't
6   know. They took away my psychology. They just took it
7   so they would like me; but they didn't. They didn't take
8   better care of me so I'm growing wings. It says so in the
9   Bible. I can. I saw it. Like Jesus did. I'm growing wings
10   and I'm going back because death people can hear the
11   real voices not from people's mouths. Like when you
12   died and I met you and called you Gabriel and you told
13   me you loved me and we made love in the Ice Cave on
14   top of the mountain, today. Do you remember? And the
15   snow swans flew with us. And we thought we could go
16   back to the world and the world will be beautiful once
17   more. But the light was dark when we sailed in and I was
18   bright but the world was dark and I tried to love everyone
19   but they couldn't see me. Then you hurt me again and
20   made me crazy. You burned me before with your hands
21   and hurt inside my bones. Remember? When Leana was
22   here? *(She is getting sleepy.)* But now I'm ready because
23   it's not my fault any more. You said you'd follow me.
24   Remember? I remember, too. And that's when you loved
25   me and not Leana.
26
27
28
29
30
31
32
33
34
35

Prodigal Kiss
by Caridad Svich

1 Marcela — late 20s	Hispanic Female — Serious

2

3   *This challenging piece describes the ordeal of fleeing Cuba in*
4   *a small boat as a refugee. Maricela is an open yet tough*
5   *young woman, whose journey across the United States will*
6   *eventually bring her to a sense of her own identity as a*
7   *person. The poetry here should not be treated as prose,*
8   *despite the "speakability" of the lines, the seeming*
9   *"naturalness" of the flow of thoughts and words. Like all fine*
10   *poetry, it offers the actress a wealth of opportunities for vocal*
11   *expressiveness, and it effectively shapes the images into*
12   *important emphases which need to be played in the*
13   *performance.*

14

15   ... There were five of us.
16   A plumber, a factory worker, a mother, her child,
17   and myself.
18   No one else. Only sea and sky.

19

20   We had food and water for two days.
21   All we had for power were oars.
22   We took turns rowing.
23   We would row for eight hours and stop.
24   If we were lucky, a current would catch us,
25   and we could rest our arms.
26   After two days, there was only a bit of water left,
27   drinking water, that is.
28   And we hadn't spotted a plane or a fishing boat
29   anywhere that could save us.

1	So we bobbed in the waves, tired of rowing,
2	and watched the sharks swim past.
3	We started praying.
4	
5	The child fed on his mother's dry tit,
6	and the plumber screamed.
7	He screamed of fire, snow, and of a head full of shit.
8	He screamed so much he couldn't get a word out.
9	After a while, his eyes became fixed. Like glass.
10	He was staring. At nothing. But he was still alive.
11	
12	The factory worker grabbed the child
13	and began to strangle it with his large hands.
14	The mother looked at him with a half-bent smile
15	and offered the factory worker her tit to suck.
16	The plumber kept staring.
17	I looked at the sky.
18	
19	It was of a deep, penetrating blue.
20	And as it grew dark, I thought I could see five moons
21	lit up at different points in the sky,
22	creating a path of light.
23	And I thought of my Santiago,
24	and how it would shine at night
25	a wash of silver hanging over
26	the cracked streets smelling of tobacco blossoms,
27	and the cheeks of children full of appetite.
28	*"Me voy pa Santiago.*
29	*Pa Santiago me voy ..."*
30	The sky turned black. For an instant.
31	And the boat swayed. I looked up again at the sky.
32	I looked for a plane that would see us and not take aim,
33	as we kept bobbing in the waves.
34	But there was nothing. Only sky.
35	

1	And I began to cast my eyes down,
2	as the factory worker tied the mother's mouth with kisses,
3	while the child hung between them like a doll,
4	grown limp and forgotten.
5	The plumber stared, and kept staring,
6	his eyes now fixed on my suitcase,
7	and I could feel the plywood and the ropes tying this mess
8	of a boat give out under the weight of the sea.
9	And that's when he fell, the staring man,
10	straight into the water, straight down.
11	And we all looked up. For a moment.
12	Catching our breath as the wind spit on the breeze.
13	
14	The factory worker let go of the mother,
15	and started cursing:
16	*"Cono carajo mierda. Cono carajo. Cono carajo."*
17	The mother looked at me.
18	She clutched my arm, digging her nails into my skin.
19	I couldn't move. I couldn't think.
20	I could only look up. And keep looking.
21	And just as my eyes were beginning to burn
22	from the heat of the sun and the sting of the air,
23	I saw a plane. A small plane flying out from under
24	some wrecking clouds.
25	And I waved with my free arm.
26	And yelled with my harsh throat.
27	And then we all started waving. Like featherless birds.
28	Waving and yelling with our mouths dry as rags,
29	and our brains drunk from the sun,
30	"Bread. Ice. Santiago ..."
31	not knowing if what we were seeing was real or imagined,
32	only knowing it was something we could recognize,
33	something that could break this prison of bobbing,
34	and waving, and looking, looking ...
35	The plane touched close. Hot metal.

1   (It was real.)

2   And slowly it lifted us up into the chill of the air.

3   And we trembled. And held our breath.

4   And kissed, kissed all that was alive in us.

5

6   And it was then that I felt I could really look

7   straight ahead without fear of what would find me,

8   for I was safe in the belly of that plane.

9   And I knew earth's will had been done.

10   Whatever else would come to me, I would no longer

11   be at the water's torturous mercy.

12

13

14

15

16

17

18

19

20

21

22

23

24

25

26

27

28

29

30

31

32

33

34

35

Prodigal Kiss
by Caridad Svich

1	Marcela — late 20s	Hispanic Female — Serious

2

3   *This is the same character as in the preceding monolog, but*
4   *in a different situation. Here she's defending herself from an*
5   *older woman who has befriended her, but who suspects*
6   *Marcela may be "soft": too naive and unable to cope with*
7   *what she'll find now that Marcela has reached the United*
8   *States. Once again, the poetry should be carefully rehearsed*
9   *so the actress can use it to exploit the images and emphases*
10 *in Marcela's thoughts. But the shape of this monolog is*
11 *different than the preceding one: the actress should note how*
12 *the defensiveness in the first part establishes a strong contrast*
13 *with the dreamlike lyricism in the final section.*

14

15 **You think I haven't been through anything?**
16 **I've been washing myself out of a bucket for ten**
17   **years,**
18 **walking on dirt roads with bare feet,**
19 **picking at wounded mangoes to eat.**
20 **Caught me a stint in prison.**
21 **Didn't do nothing 'cept disturb the peace.**
22 **That's what they called it at least.**
23 **I didn't see daylight for a year.**
24 **Nothing but a hard fixed eternity,**
25 **and shots of iodine on open skin.**
26 **And I didn't lie down then.**
27 **I kept going. Even if it was only two feet forward,**
28 **two back. I kept myself going.**
29 **'Cause I knew there was somewhere else,**

1	somewhere that was more than a spot of sand under
2	a tree.
3	I kept this letter,
4	sent to me from my Aunt Lise,
5	speaking to me about a cathedral of green.
6	And she wasn't talking about money.
7	She was talking about possibility, you see?
8	Not the kind you find on celluloid's skin,
9	but the kind that carries you
10	even if you've got no compass,
11	like the kind your father talked about
12	when he was talking about Santiago and the stars,
13	about being able to feel connected to something,
14	just by looking up into the sky.
15	And I figure if Aunt Lise found it here,
16	it's good enough for me.
17	Hell got to be better than where I've been.
18	
19	
20	
21	
22	
23	
24	
25	
26	
27	
28	
29	
30	
31	
32	
33	
34	
35	

Jambulu
by Mary Fengar Gail

1 Nella — late 20s   African Female — Serious

2

3 *Nella is a young Kenyan scientist, working on an "alien*
4 *research" project in California's Mojave Desert. She is*
5 *speaking to her project director, Dr. Judith Ambers, who has*
6 *just made insulting comments in public about the racial*
7 *inferiority of Africans. This monolog is especially challenging*
8 *because it is structured like a steadily intensifying*
9 *accusation. It has three or four sections, however, and the*
10 *actor must be able to clarify these while building to a climax.*

11

12 **My poor Africa. Nothing but bone-headed baboons with**
13 **no neurons for making radioactive waste, no neurons for**
14 **making slavery, acid rain, and two world wars! But we**
15 **students in Nairobi, we read your history, your**
16 **newspapers, and it is true we envy your stable**
17 **government, your prosperity, yet even here there are**
18 **great rifts between rich and poor, yes even here your**
19 **colored citizens must fight for their rights. Of course,**
20 **you like your weapons clean and antiseptic — state-of-**
21 **the-art technology, and you claim your wars are noble**
22 **and necessary, but you are cowardly warriors who never**
23 **see the eyes of the enemy. You push your tidy buttons**
24 **and run home claiming to have used your powers for**
25 **peace, and meanwhile you peddle your lethal wares to**
26 **poorer countries so they can kill and maim each other**
27 **in the bloody name of freedom! Democracy! Progress!**
28 **Heavens knows what great accomplishments**
29 **intelligence such as yours has given the human race:**

1   What wisdom! What goodness! What truth! What you
2   see, Doctor Ambers, are the stars, stars that are light
3   years away, but you cannot see beyond your own needle
4   nose with regard to the human race! My great
5   grandmother was born in a tin shanty in a village that
6   reeked of sewage. She lived on ungali, a corn porridge,
7   and had to wash in the river, and watch her only son go
8   begging with a wooden bowl — because he was too weak
9   to be sold to the white men running the coffee
10   plantations. To her colonialism, communism, capitalism
11   — all these were only fat words from fat books, but she
12   has endowed her sons and daughters with her wisdom,
13   her smile, and the regal bearing of a queen. There is still
14   great misery in being black — both in Africa and
15   America, and we must still rise from all the horrors of an
16   unjust past. But we will do so with dignity and strength,
17   and I would not trade my grandmother's African smile
18   for all your milky white privilege, your fat arse bank
19   accounts, and cybertechnology!
20
21
22
23
24
25
26
27
28
29
30
31
32
33
34
35

The Stonewater Rapture
by Doug Wright

1 Carlyle — 18   Female — Seriocomic

2

3 *Carlyle is a religious high school student, active in her youth*
4 *ministry group. Though her vis-à-vis is actually her*
5 *boyfriend, the actor can choose another type of listener for the*
6 *monolog in an audition situation. Carlyle never becomes*
7 *strident, even though she's indignant at what happened and*
8 *struggling to do something "adult" about it. A key to the*
9 *power in this piece is the matter-of-fact way Carlyle deals*
10 *with the problem and proposes her solution.*

11

12 Mama says you're the only decent boy for miles. She'd
13 rather talk to you than most people her own age. She
14 says boys like Arthur and Michael have one-track minds
15 that lead straight to hell, and knives where their flesh
16 should be, but not you. Which brings me to this third
17 thing on my list. Thelma Peeler. Your friend Michael
18 McCaffey took advantage of her. What's worse, he did it
19 on a dare. Arthur Horrishill took a pool, and the whole
20 team bet he couldn't do it. They ended up paying him
21 fifty dollars. It's true. He got her so drunk she didn't
22 know her own name. I know she has pimples and those
23 orthopedic shoes. But he did it just the same. Made her
24 pregnant. Michael wouldn't even offer to make it right.
25 His family just gave her family money for one of those
26 operations. Well, she wasn't about to let them kill it, so
27 she ran away and now there are patrol cars looking all
28 over the state for her. Can't you just see her clomping
29 along the roadside in those big black shoes? They'll

1   catch her in a minute and then her parents'll send her
2   back to that detention home, after they cut the baby out.
3   And it wasn't even her fault. It was his. Mama says he's
4   damned without a chance. Anyway, I think the Youth
5   Ministry should take up a collection to pay for the birth
6   of that baby.
7
8
9
10
11
12
13
14
15
16
17
18
19
20
21
22
23
24
25
26
27
28
29
30
31
32
33
34
35

Tongue of a Bird
by Ellen McLaughlin

1   Maxine — late 20s   Female — Serious
2
3   *Maxine is a search-and-rescue pilot who is really on a quest*
4   *to understand herself during her life. In this monolog she*
5   *compares her career to her personal need to search out her*
6   *own life — her own past — and "rescue" some meaning for*
7   *herself. What is especially challenging here is that the actor*
8   *must not "lose herself" in the nostalgic quality of the piece*
9   *while Maxine is reminiscing. Instead, Maxine must be seen as*
10   *struggling with her self-knowledge and with her past in order*
11   *to desperately invent something for herself to cling to in the*
12   *present. It should become the speech of an active heroine, not*
13   *that of a hesitant dreamer.*
14
15   There's a girl, this is me, standing at a high window,
16   looking down. She tells herself: You will remember this.
17   And I do. I remember everything. But I don't remember
18   why I remember this. It is morning and I'm looking down
19   across a vast landscape and I've lost something which I
20   think I will spot from this height. The farther up you are
21   the more you see. This is true, I have learned this since.
22   Because it's what I do for a living. I look, from a great
23   height, for what's been lost. I'm a pilot ... search and
24   rescue. And it's like a flicker of light sometimes,
25   perhaps the glint of a climber's goggles, the quirk,
26   almost indiscernible, of the wrong color, the dropped
27   glove, the upturned shoe. These things, the slight, the
28   rare, I see them as others don't, I am gifted — and here
29   something about this memory comes in ... A fly, I know,

1   is buzzing up the window, a trapped fly, going up the air
2   which it finds strangely hard and unyielding, going up
3   when it means to be going out. This is crucial but I don't
4   know why. Perhaps it just tells me the season, which
5   must be late autumn, a time when flies are dying in just
6   this way, going up when they mean to be going out. And
7   it seems to me that all nature is dying on this day.
8   Except me, who stands and watches ... So there's the fly
9   and there's the landscape, dropped like a platter below
10   me ... I see it as if I were above it, looking down over the
11   back of my own blond head. I see most of my past this
12   way, remembered with a detachment which looks coolly
13   down on a child I am, experiencing some dreadful thing,
14   which I experienced but didn't, and experience again in
15   recalling it, but don't. There is that girl, who is me, so
16   far below me, who might have lived my life if I hadn't left
17   her there and come up here to watch her. *(Smiles.)* I was
18   so terribly good at that. A trick I learned so early ... So
19   I became a flyer ... But she asked me to remember this.
20   So I look down with her on the bald hills of some
21   uncertain autumn, and we hear the fly and we wait.
22
23
24
25
26
27
28
29
30
31
32
33
34
35

MONOLOGS FOR MEN

Retro
by Megan Terry

1 Landy — 27   Male — Serious
2
3 *Though this speech seems intolerant and even angry on its*
4 *surface, Landy is in love with his vis-à-vis and cares deeply*
5 *for her. It's not that he resents what the stage offers her, but*
6 *more what he sees it doing to her emotionally and mentally.*
7 *The monolog offers a strong challenge for the actor to "play*
8 *opposites": to give "tough love" to the vis-à-vis. At the same*
9 *time, the piece also requires high energy from beginning to*
10 *end, because the stakes are crucially important for Landy.*
11
12 God, you're sick. I don't want you to be in that play. I've
13 never been more serious in my life. It's sick being in the
14 theater. You lay your neck on the block every time you
15 go for an audition. You're some kind of crazy masochist.
16 How can you do that to yourself? What was all the
17 anguish you were spouting about age a moment ago?
18 I'm going to make you quit that phony racket before you
19 really go crackers on me. *There's* what you should be
20 doing: writing! How long you spent on acting? How long?
21 Yeah, fifteen years. Who are you? Kids stop you for your
22 autograph? Is that the phone ringing with a movie
23 contract? Just what part do you have in this "First
24 Class" production? Do you have the first part? Are you
25 the leading woman? Are you even the second lead? Is it
26 even a good part? You are thirty years old. Just when
27 are you going to be the leading woman? When? When?
28 When?
29

Sea of Forms
by Megan Terry

1 Two — 20s	Male or Female — Seriocomic

2

3   *This monolog gives the actor a built-in vis-à-vis for strong*
4   *communication, and an exciting situation for the actor to*
5   *play. The excitement, though, shouldn't be played as a news*
6   *flash — energy should also spring from Two's enthusiasm for*
7   *the discovery that he/she is announcing. Above all, the*
8   *tender moments and humorous references should be inserted*
9   *deftly, like soft counterpoint, to the overall pace and intensity*
10 *of the main narrative.*

11

12 **Have you heard: that the latest headline from the**
13 **biology lab is a fact of exquisite beauty? Did you know**
14 **that if you allow a scientist to extract two, only two, two**
15 **out of the billions of cells in your body, to pluck these**
16 **two cells from you and place them side-by-side in a**
17 **Pyrex dish — that these two cells without a philharmonic**
18 **orchestra — that these two cells — without a conductor**
19 **— that these two cells — without the shelter of you —**
20 **that these two cells, on their own in the wide world, will**
21 **beat together in a perfect pulse. Will pulse together in a**
22 **perfect beat. As long as they are together, outside of**
23 **you on the Pyrex dish, they will beat as lovers' hearts**
24 **beat. Two together, in harmony as one. But — if you**
25 **separate these cells, and place one cell in one of your**
26 **grandmother's Pyrex dishes and the other in another**
27 **dish, they will beat separately. The same two cells from**
28 **the same body, they will beat on their own and alone.**

29

Rough Stock
by Ric Averill

1   Ray — 16   Male — Serious
2
3   *This selection should not be played with thoughtfulness and*
4   *careful remembrance. It is most effectively handled when the*
5   *young narrator is seen to struggle with the bizarre memory of*
6   *his aunt and uncle's behavior in order to make sense of it.*
7   *The actor can also use his vis-à-vis strongly here by picturing*
8   *"Viv" as an older woman to whom he wants to explain the*
9   *reasons why he left his aunt and uncle's home. Ray doesn't*
10 *reach any definite conclusion in the monolog, but he does*
11 *come to terms with sharing the painful memory with others*
12 *— a kind of reconciliation. His wonderment at the situation he*
13 *narrates, and his satisfaction at the end with having told it to*
14 *Viv, should be played strongly.*
15
16 If I have to drink every night to impress my dad I'm
17 gonna kill myself. I think it all has to do with growin' up
18 at Aunt Sally's. See, Uncle Mort and Aunt Sally had a
19 kid. He was older, adopted, not really my cousin. He was
20 Indian and kinda wild. One night we were supposed to
21 go to Victoria, to a little dance place they got? Outdoors
22 near the highway. They give concerts there. Well, I didn't
23 go. Neither did Steve — that was his name. He went
24 drinkin' with some friends and they went drag racing on
25 some country roads and they skidded out on some
26 gravel and flipped their four-wheeler. Steve died right
27 away and the kid that was driving was paralyzed ... See,
28 it wasn't so much the drinking thing — it's what
29 happened to Aunt Sally and Mort after that. See, Mort

1   took it real hard. He got lethargic, sort of drooped
2   around. The kids in the class all took up a collection to
3   make a memorial, and when they asked Uncle Mort and
4   Aunt Sally what to do with the money, Mort told them he
5   wanted a harpsichord kit. Get this — this is a country
6   boy from way back, but somewhere he's heard of some
7   Bach or Mozart or something and he wants a
8   harpsichord. So they get him the kit and he starts
9   working and keeps working and working and working.
10   You want to find Mort, he's out in the shop, working. All
11   the time. He loses his job, doesn't go in. And the
12   strange thing is, he never finished the damn thing. As far
13   as I know, he's still working on it. I don't know what he
14   does out there. And Sally, she goes over there twice a
15   week and does physical therapy on the kid. Stretches his
16   legs, pulls his arms, and she talks to him — says he
17   understands every word. He kind of grunts and moans,
18   and she's sure he lives for her visits. Can you imagine,
19   Viv? Listening to this woman who is the mother of a kid
20   who died in a car you were driving — not being able to
21   talk back or explain or apologize? *(Pause.)* Yeah, the other
22   crazy thing is, they start taking in animals, strays, until
23   the house is like a zoo. I think Sally drives around the
24   countryside looking for pets left out to die, so she can
25   bring them home and nurse them to death. I don't know.
26   I couldn't take it anymore. I hadda get out.
27
28
29
30
31
32
33
34
35

Love's Labours Wonne
by Don Nigro

1   Shakespeare — early 30s   Male — Serious

2

3   *Shakespeare here becomes a dark, manic genius whose*
4   *thoughts erupt in sudden, powerful flashes. The performer*
5   *can use the monolog to good advantage since it refers to*
6   *locations on a theatrical stage in the first section. The piece*
7   *also offers the actor a wide range of unique choices for strong*
8   *emotions towards the theatre, audiences and directors.*

9

10   **When I was young I dreamed of this. The Globe's a little**
11   **world of looking glass in which I see dark fantasies of**
12   **violence and lechery played out for me. Up in the loft,**
13   **the pigeon-haunted heaven peopled mostly by**
14   **musicians, an unrealistic touch. The boards on which I**
15   **walk are earth and do have worms. Verisimilitude. Down**
16   **in the spidered trap is hell, it's cold, but lovely rats. A**
17   **tidy Christian world in which to smear myself with pagan**
18   **metaphor and play out mindless rituals. But safe. I've**
19   **built a universe of lies, all this is nothing. I am terrified**
20   **of nothing, why won't my hand stop shaking? When the**
21   **gun misfired in *Tamburlaine* and killed the pregnant**
22   **woman in the audience, now there was theatre! There**
23   **was a working metaphor, something done. I hate you**
24   **people. Cannibals. God eats the children of my flesh,**
25   **you eat the children of my soul. This place is dressed in**
26   **lies and made of death, the substance of this place is**
27   **death. I rot and rot and thereby hangs the tale.**

28

29

Abingdon Square
by Maria Irene Fornés

1 Michael — 24   Male — Serious
2
3 *This powerful monolog is spoken to Michael's stepmother —*
4 *who is the same age as he — and whom he has discovered*
5 *having an affair with a younger man. Michael is torn between*
6 *the love he feels towards his father and the rapport he has*
7 *discovered with Marion: should he reveal the affair to his*
8 *father and betray Marion? or conceal the affair and betray his*
9 *parent? And although the monolog reads as though Michael*
10 *has made a decision, it's best to play it as though he's*
11 *thinking through all sides of the dilemma in order to discover*
12 *the right course of action for himself.*
13
14 When I'm with him I care about nothing but him. I love
15 him. He's my father and I love him. And I don't want to
16 see him suffer. When I'm with you I forget that he's my
17 father and I take your side. He's my father and I love
18 him and I respect him. And I feel terrible that I've been
19 disloyal to him. And I feel worse to see that he's still
20 gentle and kind to both you and me. I'm sorry because
21 I love you too, and I know that you too need me. But I
22 can't bear being divided, and I have to choose him. I'm
23 leaving, Marion. I can't remain here any longer knowing
24 what I know and feeling what I do about it. It's too
25 painful and I'm demeaned by my betrayal of him. There
26 are times when I want to tell him the whole truth. And
27 if I don't, it's because I love you too and I feel there's no
28 wrong in what you're doing. I really don't. I think you're
29 right in what you're doing. You're young and you're in

1   love and it's a person's right to love. I think so. Frank
2   is handsome and I think he is honest. I mean, I think he
3   loves you. He's not very strong, but he's young. No one
4   is strong when he's young. I'm not. Only I'm still playing
5   with soldiers and he's entered into the grown-up world.
6   If I were in his place, it would terrify me to be the lover
7   of a married woman. Good-bye, my sister. I must leave.
8   I am constantly forced to act in a cowardly manner. I
9   cannot be loyal to both, and I cannot choose one over
10   the other, and I feel a coward when I look at you, and I
11   feel a coward when I look at him. I am tearing out my
12   heart and leaving it here, as half of it is yours, and the
13   other half is his. I hope I won't hurt you by leaving —
14   besides missing me, which I know you will. I mean
15   beyond that. I mean that I hope my leaving has no
16   consequences beyond our missing each other. Take care.
17
18
19
20
21
22
23
24
25
26
27
28
29
30
31
32
33
34
35

Souvenirs
by Sheldon Rosen

1	Peter — 28	Black Male — Serious
2		

3 *In this monolog Peter speaks feelingly of his island culture to*
4 *a white man whom he knows will never understand him.*
5 *He's warning his vis-à-vis of imminent danger in this foreign*
6 *place. The speech should be played with strong belief, as*
7 *well as mystery and secrecy. It can also tolerate an occasional*
8 *note of dark humor which is subtle, but a challenge to play.*
9 *All this is difficult to achieve without allowing the urgency*
10 *of the situation to sag, but the selection is relatively short and*
11 *gives the actor good opportunity to shape it effectively.*
12
13 **It is everybody's cause! Everything is connected, don't**
14 **you know that? Just like the wave that comes here to**
15 **the shore is connected to the wave out there in the**
16 **ocean thousands of miles away. I know that as a fact.**
17 **What we burn here is carried in the wind to your soil.**
18 **What is murdered here will haunt your lives the same**
19 **way! There is someone you should meet. My friend,**
20 **Medwin. It was his idea that I talk to you. Medwin will**
21 **be able to convince you. He taught me that to care**
22 **about other people was not only good, it was smart. He**
23 **said not caring was a disease that was sweeping the**
24 **world and that there would be so much not caring going**
25 **on that the earth itself would stop caring one day and**
26 **wouldn't turn around the sun any longer. Medwin, he's**
27 **going to be the savior of this island.**
28
29

The China Crisis
by Kipp Erante Cheng

1   Mickey Finn — 30s   Male — Comic

2

3   *This tongue-in-cheek piece capitalizes upon the stereotype of*

4   *the "private eye" made famous in American folklore by*

5   *countless "tough guy" characters in forties radio dramas and*

6   *crime movies — perhaps best typified by Humphrey Bogart in*

7   *THE MALTESE FALCON. Here, Mickey Finn, Private*

8   *Investigator, enters. He wears a trench coat, a hat, and a*

9   *dead-pan, tough-guy smirk. He speaks into a hand-held tape*

10   *recorder.*

11

12   **Reminder: Time to quit the smokes. Dolores, remind me**

13   **to quit the smokes. And get a pound of Java, ground**

14   **extra fine. And some kitty litter for the cat.** *(Beat.)* **And**

15   **some flowers for the old lady.** *(FINN lights another*

16   *cigarette, then turns to address the audience.)* **The name's**

17   **Finn. Mickey Finn. Private Investigator. I usually do the**

18   **kind of paper-pushing work that doesn't amount to a hill**

19   **a beans in a city like New York. Divorce surveillance.**

20   **Insurance fraud. Cases with simple solutions and happy**

21   **endings. It was two-thirty in the** A.M. **I was standing**

22   **outside of the Golden Chopstix, a sleazy dive in the**

23   **heart of old Chinatown. Great Hunan egg rolls. But**

24   **forget the Moo Goo Gai Pan. This was the kind of**

25   **restaurant that invented the phrase MSG reaction. After**

26   **a long night of sneaking around in dark alleys and hiding**

27   **under beds, all a guy wants to do is pick up some**

28   **Chinese take-out, go back to the flea-bag that he calls**

29   **home, and listen to some Glenn Gould until the liquor**

1   takes hold. Or at least until his girl calls, looking to
2   acquire company. Or until morning comes and
3   everything starts all over again. *(FINN puts out his*
4   *cigarette.)* **Gotta quit these things. Soon. The trouble is,**
5   **the taste gets under your skin.** Every drag reminds you
6   of some girl in a bar, singing a sad song, singing the
7   song as if you're the only chump around. As if she's
8   singing the song just for you. Cigarettes are like Chinese
9   food. You have one and then half an hour later your
10   fingers are itching to get hold of another precious coffin
11   nail. *(Beat.)* **I guess that's just the nature of addiction.**
12
13
14
15
16
17
18
19
20
21
22
23
24
25
26
27
28
29
30
31
32
33
34
35

Final Passages
by Robert Schenkkan

1   Tom — 20s   Male — Serious

2

3   *This monolog challenges the actor to create a strong sense of*
4   *mood as he recalls the nightmare of helplessly witnessing a*
5   *tragedy taking place. The actor must avoid the trap of*
6   *allowing the character's memories to dampen the*
7   *performance. Careful attention to pace is therefore important,*
8   *as well as Tom's need to win understanding of his vis-à-vis.*
9   *The short and choppy sentences should be used energetically*
10 *to reveal Tom's fears and desperate need to sort out his*
11 *tangled emotions.*

12

13 **When I was ten I watched a loose team of horses**
14 **trample a little girl to death. Hot, bright day. Sun so**
15 **sharp it'd peel your scalp back like a razor. No wind. Air**
16 **heavy. Breath hard, I'm sittin' on the sidewalk. Back**
17 **pressed hard into a brick wall. Tryin' to wrap a little**
18 **shadow over me. Sweat gluin' my shirt to the brick.**
19 **Nine, ten feet from me, there's a little brown girl in the**
20 **mud. Buildin' little mounds, then laughin', squealin', as**
21 **she kicks 'em to pieces. Across the street, old man**
22 **rearrangin' the fruit outside his store. Peels an orange.**
23 **Eats it. I watch the juice drop down his chin. Little girl's**
24 **mother leans out a window. Yells at her to come in.**
25 **Little girl ignores her. I feel it first. Runnin' up my spine.**
26 **The sidewalk starts to shake, hums like a sheet about**
27 **to snap. Then I hear it. Real low at first. A crazy**
28 **poundin', yellin'. Then they're there. Right there.**
29 **Roundin' the corner. A team of four big dray horses,**

1   lashed to an empty wagon. Spooked, runnin' scared.
2   Manes whippin' back. All hoofs and wild eyes and spit.
3   Throwin' up the ground behind 'em like a black cloud. We
4   all watchin': me, the old man, the woman at the window,
5   the little girl. Everythin' just stops. Still. Stops. Nobody
6   moves. Nobody yells. And then they're past. Racin' down
7   the street. Out of sight. Just a faint rumble. Then
8   nothin'. Just quiet. Nothin'. The little girl is gone.
9   Complete gone. Like she's never been there. The woman
10   at the window starts to cry. I hear flies. Even when I
11   knew, I couldn't stop it. Couldn't stop things. Like those
12   horses ... like what I did. Couldn't stop it. Couldn't stop it.
13
14
15
16
17
18
19
20
21
22
23
24
25
26
27
28
29
30
31
32
33
34
35

Sunday Sermon
by David Henry Hwang

1   Minister — 28   Male — Comic

2

3   *The context of this darkly humorous monolog is a church*
4   *service and the vis-à-vis is the congregation — a situation that*
5   *allows the actor to play the speech directly to the audience.*
6   *Another unique feature of this piece is that it permits extreme*
7   *rhetorical gestures and vocal interpretation, prodding the*
8   *actor to exploit the language to its full extent. Needless to say,*
9   *the Minister must be played seriously in order for the humor*
10   *to emerge.*

11

12   We thank the choir for that inspiring and enthusiastic
13   rendition. Today's choice of anthem seems particularly
14   appropriate in view of today's sermon topic: "How to
15   Spread the Gospel in the Event of Nuclear War." I know
16   there are people who would rather we shy away from the
17   tough decisions every Christian must make once the
18   bombs hit the ground. I do not count myself among
19   them. Many of us have been conditioned to stereotype a
20   nuclear holocaust as a bad thing. This is simply narrow
21   minded. A nuclear war can be a great tragedy or a great
22   opportunity, a vehicle for Satan or for the soldiers of
23   righteousness. If we don't reap the harvest of such an
24   event, you can be sure that scores of Satan's little
25   workers will be out sowing the seeds of evil, out
26   amongst the maimed and wounded, enslaving them to
27   illicit drugs, performing abortions, teaching evolution,
28   and encouraging positive portrayals of homosexuals on
29   our television networks. What a difference a nuclear war

1   will make for us, the soul winners! No more houses of
2   prostitution, no more ERA, no more drugs, no more Kurt
3   Vonnegut! Gone will be gun control laws, homosexual
4   housing ordinances, busing, and teenage free clinics!
5   And we will be able to start once again, hand-in-hand to
6   re-create the world envisioned by the founding fathers: a
7   nation of free men, mule and woman by their side,
8   working the land with their hands and organizing
9   television boycotts! When we look at it this way, is a
10   nuclear holocaust all that bad?
11
12
13
14
15
16
17
18
19
20
21
22
23
24
25
26
27
28
29
30
31
32
33
34
35

Principia Scriptoriae
by Richard Nelson

1 Ernesto — 20s   Hispanic Male — Seriocomic

2

3 *This monolog is edited together from a two-character scene,*
4 *so an auditionee should add reactions from the vis-à-vis in*
5 *order to motivate the changing attitudes of Ernesto. He is a*
6 *man feeling out of place in Britain, as the monolog explains.*
7 *The speech is rich in reactions and changes of mood as*
8 *Ernesto describes studying at a famous university.*

9

10 You know, it's not at all like everyone says it is —
11 Cambridge, Bill, English universities in general, actually.
12 Oxbridge, I mean. They're not all homosexual. Everyone
13 said they were — before I left. Everyone who talked to
14 my mother did. You wouldn't believe the bizarre
15 conversations my mother and I had before I left. It's not
16 often that a son gets such a clear picture of just how
17 his mother's mind works. There is a good reason for
18 that. There is a human reason for that. Here is this nice
19 upper-middle class lady — and what does she start to
20 do: take her only son around to brothels. Mind you, the
21 better brothels, but still. I'm not saying she went in. God
22 forbid. She just took me around. She stayed outside.
23 She just hung around outside. And paid. This is true.
24 There can be some really strange shit down here. People
25 can be really screwed up down here. She'd pay and stay
26 outside. But first they'd have to haggle, though. I'm
27 standing there and they are haggling over the price. My
28 mother and the prostitute. That sort of does something
29 to one's sense of pride. And none of it would have

1   happened if the priest hadn't told her about English
2   universities. The ideas that people get into their head.
3
4
5
6
7
8
9
10
11
12
13
14
15
16
17
18
19
20
21
22
23
24
25
26
27
28
29
30
31
32
33
34
35

The Fifth Sun
by Nicholas A. Patricca

1   Colonel — 28   Hispanic Male — Serious

2

3   *This frightening monolog is spoken by a Central American*
4   *military officer who leads death squads in his country — often*
5   *against high-ranking members of the clergy who oppose the*
6   *government, as is the case here. Because of its power the*
7   *speech doesn't need to be "overplayed" by the actor; the real*
8   *horror of such ideas is their matter-of-fact quality — they are*
9   *perfectly natural and believable to those who express them.*
10   *The piece is challenging, though, because the rhetoric of the*
11   *speech moves step-by-step up the ladder towards its chilling*
12   *conclusion.*

13

14   Patriots! A dark cancer gnaws at the heart of our nation!
15   Like a giant octopus its black tentacles creep into every
16   sector of our society. This black beast is eating away
17   the moral fiber of our youth. It seduces them with so-
18   called humanitarian ideas. In the name of human rights
19   and social justice, it perverts their natural idealism for
20   unnatural ends. What do you see? Do you see a man? a
21   strong, virile man? a true son of El Salvador? No! You
22   see a drug addict, a homosexual, an internationalist. He
23   has deceived Rome! He has deceived Washington! But
24   he has not deceived us. We, the White Warriors, are not
25   deceived by these false Christians, these castrated men
26   and women in black robes who are making our children
27   soft and effeminate, robbing them of their manhood and
28   of their birthright, making them soft clay to be molded
29   into socialist slaves by their red masters. We must fight

1   this black beast! We are the surgeons of Christ. We must
2   act now to cut out this corruption from our body. We are
3   men! We do not wait for others to tell us what to do! This
4   is our country! These are our children! We are the true
5   sons and fathers of El Salvador! BE A PATRIOT, KILL A
6   PRIEST! BE A PATRIOT, KILL A NUN! Sever the hands
7   and feet of this black monster! Then I shall squash its
8   helpless head under the heels of my boots!
9
10
11
12
13
14
15
16
17
18
19
20
21
22
23
24
25
26
27
28
29
30
31
32
33
34
35

The Fifth Sun
by Nicholas A. Patricca

1   Rutilio — 28   Hispanic Male — Serious
2
3   *This peasant-priest is torn between his loyalty to the Christian*
4   *ideal of nonviolence and the outrage he feels when*
5   *confronting social injustice in Central America. He must also*
6   *confront his own violent tendencies here, which is the*
7   *monolog's real source of power.*
8
9   Monseñor, I have chosen never to touch a gun. But I can
10   understand why a brother priest might choose
11   otherwise. In the mountains once, I got lost. I came
12   upon this large hut. But there were six coffins in it. They
13   were simple coffins like we use all the time, except they
14   each had this little hole in the lid with a drinking straw
15   in it. There was this terrible odor. Then I heard this
16   sound. It seemed to come from one of the coffins. I went
17   over. The stench made me very sick. I heard this sound
18   again. I tried to open the lid, it was nailed down very
19   tight. I got some tools from my jeep. Inside each coffin
20   was a living corpse, a living dead man. Those thugs
21   from Orden had kept them alive, to torture them. They
22   fed them a little atole every day just to torture them. I
23   went to get some help. There was nothing we could do.
24   Their bodies ... We had to let them die. Monseñor, I
25   wanted to kill those bastards from Orden. I wanted to
26   kill them. And I wanted to kill those poor people in the
27   coffins to put them out of their misery. And I wanted to
28   kill myself too. Sometimes my doubts are stronger than
29   my faith.

The Migrant Farmworker's Son
by Silvia Gonzalez S.

1   DAD — 30s   Hispanic Male — Serious
2
3   *This moving speech has a clear vis-à-vis: the son who has*
4   *misunderstood his father throughout the play and to whom*
5   *the father must now finally explain himself — his temper*
6   *flashes, his seeming hostility to his son, his depression and*
7   *desperate clinging to the past life and customs the family left*
8   *behind in Mexico. What is at stake is nothing less than the*
9   *love or the hatred of his young son. Although the monolog*
10 *occurs only at the very end of the play (and hence, the pent-*
11 *up emotions have been well-prepared), an actor can deliver it*
12 *effectively as an audition piece without such preparation. It*
13 *demands strong identification with the situation of the father,*
14 *and an absolute commitment to the need the father has for*
15 *reconciliation with his only surviving child whom he has*
16 *alienated for so many years.*
17
18 If you ever want to kill me, I give you permission. Why
19 would I want to live anyway? I'm no good. I hurt the
20 people I love. I can't give you a better life. I am ashamed
21 of myself at every turn. I make mistakes every single
22 day. The picture is the next beautiful thing to your
23 mother. I never wanted to tell you about this because I
24 didn't want you to suffer like me ... *(Pause.)* You and your
25 mother have a connection I envy. We wanted two
26 children. A son for her and a daughter for me. We had
27 made plans to spoil each one in our own private way.
28 Then she went away ... I had the love of a daughter and
29 she went away. She is your sister. One year after you

1 were born, she was taken away from me. From your
2 mother and I. I have not been able to forget her. Do you
3 know what kind of pain is in your stomach when you see
4 a child you've given life to sink to the bottom of the
5 water? ... No. You don't understand my pain. No one
6 does. Your mother is a strong woman and she let God
7 have her fifteen years ago. But I couldn't let her go. I
8 want to hold her every day. I want to touch her hair and
9 the ruffles on her dress. I DIDN'T GET A CHANCE TO
10 LOVE HER ... To think she would have been married by
11 now. *(HENRY has been retreating.)* I blame myself. I am a
12 stupid man.... Come back here with your belt and "dame
13 shingasos." I deserve it for what I have done to you. I let
14 misery take me away. This house and the one in Salinas
15 have had misery imprinted on the walls. It's time to
16 wash it away.
17
18
19
20
21
22
23
24
25
26
27
28
29
30
31
32
33
34
35

The Emerald Circle
by Max Bush

1   Dave — Teens   Male — Serious

2

3   *In this monolog Dave tries to explain his terrible fears to his*

4   *best friend and his mother. He has just lost his temper during*

5   *a backyard basketball game with his friend and started a fist-*

6   *fight, even threatening his mother while "out of control." Here*

7   *Dave reveals how he was shamed recently in front of his*

8   *girlfriend Sandy by a strange, older bully. It happened one*

9   *night in the cemetery where Dave and Sandy were meeting,*

10   *and Dave was helpless to prevent the bully from dragging*

11   *Sandy off with him. Dave has been silent around the house*

12   *and at school since the incident, and this is where he first*

13   *begins to "open up" and tell others about the incident.*

14

15   I keep seeing that night over and over again. I hear him.

16   It's like he's right here, right next to me, talking to me,

17   talking. I can't shut him up. And I dream about her. I'm

18   underground, hiding or dead or something, and I can't

19   breathe. I can't push the ground off me. I can't move. I

20   keep looking for that guy. I even think I see him

21   sometimes and I get ready and it's not him. Everywhere

22   I go I think he's watching me. You can't see at night.

23   Like at the movies, tonight. He could just come up,

24   come up out of nowhere again. So I got to stay ready, I

25   got to be ready this time. I want a gun. I think about a

26   gun all the time. Then I'd be ready. Then that crazy

27   bastard wouldn't get away. But I — I can't trust myself.

28   I'll shoot somebody else, I know I will. I hit you, didn't

29   I? I hit you! So a knife, I'll carry a knife — and —and I

1   do, all the time. I have a knife. But they don't let you
2   have a knife in school and I know he was there, he was
3   watching Sandy there, at school. He was watching us all
4   over. He called her by her name. And me. He called me
5   by my name, too. He was watching me, too. I wish he'd
6   come back. I even went out to the cemetery looking for
7   him, calling for him, but he wasn't there. I'm sorry I hit
8   you. You can hit me back; I won't do anything. I'm sorry
9   I hit you.
10
11
12
13
14
15
16
17
18
19
20
21
22
23
24
25
26
27
28
29
30
31
32
33
34
35

Heaven's Hard
by Jordan Budde

1   Bo — 28   Male — Serious

2

3   *This is a stepping-stone monolog that builds rapidly at the*
4   *end; and one that contains a clearly defined vis-à-vis, offering*
5   *a wide range of choices for the actor. It's especially*
6   *challenging because it requires that the actor become truly*
7   *inspired and unafraid of the lyricism occurring near the end.*
8   *The religious excitement can't be faked, nor can the touching*
9   *relationship between Bo and his mother that the monolog*
10   *reflects.*

11

12   You know what I did today, mama? Just for you? I drove
13   over to our church — your church, mama. I went inside
14   — I was the only one there. You told me that was where
15   I should look for God. So I looked. I yelled. "Hey God,
16   I'm here!" I hate that church. You always making me go.
17   Wantin' everyone to see us. I sat down. It was so quiet.
18   The pews in that church — all facing forward in those
19   long, ordered rows — each row a tiny bit higher than the
20   one in front of it — giving that whole room the feelin' of
21   movin' forward. Remember how the ushers would come
22   and once a row was all full up they would close those
23   little wooden doors on the end of each row — just like
24   you were getting on a roller coaster. That big roller
25   coaster at the state fair. "Put on your seat belts, folks,
26   hold on tight!" I'm surprised those ushers didn't yell out
27   that. But then ... ha! Nothing! Nothing happened! I was
28   ready to go places! Feeeeeel something! But your
29   preacher — he just stood there, droning on about

1 nothing, smiling through coffee-stained teeth, asking for
2 money, leading the congregation as they sang some
3 song from another century! He had no more light in his
4 eye than a statue — a dead stone statue covered in
5 pigeon shit! It was like going to the fair and getting on
6 the roller coaster and never movin' an inch! If I had a
7 church, it would MOVE! You'd come in, sit down and you
8 better damn well believe you'd need a seat belt! I'd fly
9 you right by the door to heaven, all the songs would be
10 new and beautiful — breathtaking! Joy would be
11 overflowing in your heart! There'd be love in that room,
12 like a warm wave moving back and forth ... You'd walk
13 out of my church new, bright and confident — with a
14 suntan on your face from gettin' so close to the holy
15 presence of God!
16
17
18
19
20
21
22
23
24
25
26
27
28
29
30
31
32
33
34
35

4 Square Blocks
by Michelle A. Hamilton

| 1 | Gabe — 30s | Male — Seriocomic |

3   *Gabe is a down-and-out writer and a kind of philosopher. His*
4   *story of the plant is plainly a ladder-type of speech, reaching*
5   *a climax (and moral point) at the end just as the vine or plant*
6   *does. The challenge for the actor in this piece is to avoid*
7   *"playing the end from the beginning": to tell the story*
8   *moment-by-moment as if Gabe himself doesn't yet realize the*
9   *full "meaning" or "lesson" that his plant has to teach.*
10 *Discovery and surprise are all-important in performing this*
11 *monolog. One final point: most of the lapses in the text here*
12 *(indicated by elision) are places where the other character's*
13 *questions or statements have been edited out.*

15 **You sure? ... I wouldn't wanna bore you ... You like**
16 **hearing me talk? ... Okay. So this plant, Monstera**
17 **deliciosa, besides having a cool sounding Latin name,**
18 **lives way way up in the tree canopy, like hundreds of**
19 **feet up in the air, but, it doesn't start there. It starts on**
20 **the ground like all normal plants. So the Momma plant**
21 **way up in the tree branches, drops a fruit and it falls to**
22 **the ground and rots, and the seeds, hundreds of them,**
23 **eventually push their way up outa the soil towards the**
24 **light. Like normal seeds, right? ... Wrong. You see, once**
25 **these little baby seedlings break outa the soil they do**
26 **something different. Insteada growing up towards the**
27 **sun, they stretch and grow towards the deepest**
28 **darkness they can find ... That's what I'm telling you.**
29 **Different. Unusual. So, there they are, stretching out**

1   towards the deepest darkness, like hundreds of long
2   white threads, you see, they don't got any leaves yet,
3   they're just threads ... No leaves. Not yet ... So the few
4   seedling threads that chose well, that chose to grow in
5   the right direction and were lucky enough to locate a
6   tree within their given six feet, they, those happy well
7   choosing few, finally get to grow towards the sun ... The
8   ones that make it to a tree don't die. But they change.
9   They start growing up the tree and towards the sun and
10 you know what? They grow leaves. They grow up the
11 tree putting out more and more and bigger and bigger
12 leaves. The thin white little thread getting bigger and
13 stronger as the plant vines and climbs its way outa the
14 darkness and into the light ... So far we just got a vine
15 with little heart-shaped leaves and this plant don't look
16 like that, right? That's because it ain't done changing
17 yet. It ain't home yet. Remember? Its real home is way,
18 way up in the jungle canopy, not in the darkness of the
19 ground and not as a vine clinging to a trunk, but
20 perched up on a branch of a tall tall tree. So, when it
21 gets there, gets home, it changes again! Three changes.
22 From the thread in the darkness, to the vine on the tree,
23 to this. This Monstera deliciosa Swiss Cheese plant. In
24 fact, the vine that got it there, way up there in the sky?
25 It withers and dies. But that's okay 'cause sometimes
26 the things which get you out of the darkness you don't
27 need anymore once you get in the light. Know what I
28 mean?
29
30
31
32
33
34
35

Les Trois Dumas
by Charles Smith

1   Alexandre — 20s   African-American Male — Serious

2

3   *This mocking diatribe is delivered by Alexandre Dumas fils to*

4   *his father, the great French nineteenth-century author,*

5   *Alexandre Dumas pére. The older Dumas was noted for*

6   *leading a scandalous life in Paris, a fact which only seemed*

7   *to heighten the popularity of his plays and novels such as*

8   *The Man In the Iron Mask, The Three Musketeers, and*

9   *others. In the play, young Alexandre is a bitter, self-hating*

10   *moralist, obsessed by his family's tortured African-American*

11   *history. In this speech he contemplates the disgusting*

12   *possibility that his parent may actually be honored by one of*

13   *France's most distinguished bodies of public and literary*

14   *taste, the French Academy. All the resentment and frustration*

15   *Alexandre feels towards his father openly explodes in this*

16   *climactic speech, loaded with strong conflicts.*

17

18   **The Academy is to open its ranks to you? The Academy**

19   **will never induct you. Victor Hugo, maybe, but you,**

20   **never. If the Academy were a popularity contest, you**

21   **would have been inducted years ago. But it is not a**

22   **popularity contest. The Academy maintains standards**

23   **of literary taste, and when it comes to taste, literary or**

24   **otherwise, you just don't have any. Your morals are in a**

25   **shambles. You move from seamstress, to courtesan, to**

26   **actress without any regard as to the consequences of**

27   **your liaisons. Victor Hugo, on the other hand, is a family**

28   **man of high morals and unreproachable ethics. Victor**

29   **Hugo can be seen most any day strolling down the**

1   avenue with his wife and children. You don't have a wife
2   and I doubt if you're even aware of how many children
3   you have. The way you've spread your seed around only
4   God knows how many children you really have. I may
5   have brothers and sisters all over Paris. I've made it into
6   a bit of a game, actually, as I walk down the avenue. I
7   always search the eyes of strangers looking for hints of
8   recognition. A sparkle in the eye. A curl in the corner of
9   the lip. Or perhaps a distinctive swagger in the way one
10   walks, who knows when I may stumble upon the
11   remnants of one of your illicit liaisons? Is it your
12   intention to ridicule all of France by suggesting that the
13   Academy would open its arms to the likes of you?
14   That's a fiction more outrageous than one of your
15   novels. It will never happen. It will not.
16
17
18
19
20
21
22
23
24
25
26
27
28
29
30
31
32
33
34
35

Brown & Black & White All Over
by Antonio Sacre

1 Thomas — 20s   Male or Female — Seriocomic

2

3 *This piece offers a wealth of possibilities for physical and*
4 *vocal interpretation. Although the story belongs to an*
5 *indigenous American storytelling tradition, it can be*
6 *presented by an actor of any ethnic background, and by an*
7 *actor of either sex (in the original one-person show, the*
8 *"character" is a short white Irish male). It's also possible to*
9 *edit the piece handily to a shorter length, if needed, by*
10 *cutting the last eight lines, while still retaining much of the*
11 *integrity of the original. (Special pronunciations: Tecuziztecatl*
12 *= "The-koo-zees-TEK-attle." Nanahuaitzin = "Na-na-WATTS-*
13 *zin." Mexica = "Meh-SHEEK-ah.")*

14

15 Once upon a time, once over time, once under time,
16 once in a time before time was put on little watches and
17 worn on wrists, in other words, a long time ago, the
18 Gods met in what is now called Mexico long before it
19 was called Mexico, and they decided to make the sun
20 and the moon. So they built a huge fire and they knew
21 that somebody needed to jump in that fire and get the
22 sun, and carry it up on those flames into the sky. So one
23 of the gods stepped forward. He was a tall god, a
24 handsome god, the richest god, he said my name is
25 Tecuziztecatl. I am the tallest god. I am the handsomest
26 god. I am the richest god. I deserve to be the sun. I will
27 jump into the flames. And the gods were impressed.
28 Now they needed the moon. One of the smallest gods,
29 one of the ugliest gods, one of the poorest gods stepped

1   forward and said my name is Nanahuaitzin, which
2   means face covered with festering boils. I am the
3   shortest god. I am the ugliest god. I am the poorest god.
4   I will jump in the fire and become the moon. And so the
5   gods began to play their drums and sing the songs of
6   the sun and the songs of the moon, and the two gods
7   stepped toward the flame, and Tecuziztecatl put his
8   hand in front of Nanahuaitzin and said, I go first. And
9   he walked toward the flame and when he felt the heat
10   on his face, he stepped back. And a second time he
11   leaned into the flame and a second time he leaned back.
12   A third time he leaned even closer and saw the sparks
13   shooting into the sky and he was scared and a third
14   time he stepped back, and a fourth time he tried, these
15   things happen in fours I don't know why, and a fourth
16   time he was a coward. And the drumming stopped, and
17   the gods whispered, and in the confusion Nanahuaitzin
18   ran as fast as his little legs could carry him and jumped
19   as high as he could and in a shower of sparks he was
20   gone. Tecuziztecatl took courage from that and jumped
21   in too. The gods waited to see who would come up first,
22   the sun or the moon. Well, Nanahuaitzin came up first,
23   but when he was in the fire, he didn't choose the moon,
24   the little shit, he chose the sun, and Tecuziztecatl took
25   what was left, and when he came up in the sky as the
26   moon he was mad, and he screamed at Nanahuaitzin,
27   give me back the sun. I deserve to be the sun, I am the
28   richest and handsomest god, give me the sun and
29   Nanahuaitzin was silent. He yelled down to the gods,
30   make him give me the sun! They said no. You do not
31   deserve the sun. You were not brave when you should
32   have been, and even though you were handsome and
33   rich on earth, you will not be so in the sky. You will be
34   paler than the sun, and on certain nights you will be full,
35   and on other nights you will be half full, on other nights

1   you will be a mere sliver of yourself, and on other nights
2   you will not even be seen at all. And Nanahuaitzin, even
3   though you were the poorest thing on earth, in the sky
4   you will be the brightest most amazing thing. And so it
5   remains to this day. But they had a problem.
6   Nanahuaitzin was not moving in the sky. They asked,
7   please, Nanahuaitzin, move or we will all burn here on
8   the earth, and Nanahuaitzin remained silent. They
9   pleaded, and still he said nothing. They said they would
10   all die and a third time he was silent. A fourth time they
11   asked and the fourth time is a magic number in these
12   stories I don't know why. The fourth time they asked,
13   Nanahuaitzin said I will not move unless the rest of you
14   throw yourselves into the fire as well. And they knew he
15   was right. And they all jumped in the fire, and the sun
16   began to move. Out of the fire jumped the Mexica
17   people. We call them Mexicans now, and they knew to
18   keep the sun moving in the sky, they had to make
19   sacrifices.
20
21
22
23
24
25
26
27
28
29
30
31
32
33
34
35

The Last Magician
by Albert Morell

1	Bennett — Indeterminate Age

1   Bennett — Indeterminate Age   Male — Serious

2

3   *This stepping-stone type of monolog contains flashes of*

4   *impatience and sarcasm, especially at the beginning, and it*

5   *gradually develops several climaxes before its final powerful*

6   *declaration of Bennett's atheism. Like the earlier monolog*

7   *from THE LAST MAGICIAN, this one also invites the actor to*

8   *stretch his imaginative resources in portraying a*

9   *contemporary character rich in spiritual dimensions. Bennett,*

10   *like Crowley, is an eminently theatrical "character."*

11

12   **Your intellectual snobbery is shallow and foolish,**

13   **Aleister. The initiate must be drilled in the most**

14   **rudimentary elements. There's more opportunity for**

15   **error in the practice of Magick than in any other branch**

16   **of physics. And it's a hell of a sight more dangerous.**

17   **Shallow critics argue that spirits don't exist because the**

18   **average untrained man cannot evoke them, or that the**

19   **ritual used to conjure them is nonsense. A scientist's**

20   **electroscope would be useless in the hands of a savage.**

21   **You don't want to remain a savage all your life, do you?**

22   **I know I'll die if I don't get out of London to a warmer**

23   **climate. Death doesn't bother me. It's a cleaner**

24   **business than birth. One day when I was sixteen, the**

25   **conversation turned to childbirth. What I heard**

26   **disgusted me. I became furiously angry and said that**

27   **children are brought to earth by angels. The next day**

28   **one of the boys brought an illustrated manual of**

29   **obstetrics and I could not doubt the facts. I thought if**

1	God invented so degrading a way to perpetuate the
2	species, then he must be a devil delighting in
3	loathsomeness. From that moment I no longer believed
4	in the existence of God. Some are born on this planet at
5	home in the flesh. Others, like me, remain disembodied
6	all their lives. Maybe this is what drew me to Magick.
7	
8	
9	
10	
11	
12	
13	
14	
15	
16	
17	
18	
19	
20	
21	
22	
23	
24	
25	
26	
27	
28	
29	
30	
31	
32	
33	
34	
35	

The Last Magician
by Albert Morell

1   Aleister Crowley — 20s   Male — Serious

2

3   *This is a ladder-type monolog that has a strongly defined vis-*

4   *à-vis whom the actor can easily imagine giving reactions to*

5   *Crowley's statements. The historical character is not a*

6   *religious fanatic: he seriously believes all that he's saying*

7   *and he passionately defends himself as he tries to convince*

8   *Ivor about the value of his beliefs.*

9

10   **What is it you want to do eventually, Ivor? I'd like to be**

11   **a famous poet and join the diplomatic corps as well.**

12   **But suppose I make a great success in diplomacy and**

13   **become ambassador to Paris? What's the good in that?**

14   **How many people can so much as remember the name**

15   **of the ambassador a hundred years ago? So far as being**

16   **a poet, out of the three thousand men in residence, how**

17   **many know anything about so great a man as**

18   **Aeschylus? A mere fraction. Even if I did more than**

19   **Caesar or Napoleon or Homer or Shakespeare, my work**

20   **would disappear when the earth becomes uninhabitable**

21   **for men. I want to do something that will survive. I want**

22   **an immortality which reaches beyond the dimensions of**

23   **this world — that of a Magician. Never mind, I knew**

24   **you'd laugh, but not that kind of a magician, you idiot.**

25   **The kind that investigates the hidden mysteries. I want**

26   **to experience everything without distinguishing between**

27   **good and evil. Do you believe in God, Ivor? Then you**

28   **must believe in the existence of non-material**

29   **dimensions populated by intelligent beings, say spirits,**

1	angels, demons, the earth's dead. Well, I want to find out
2	how these other realities are structured. How these
3	beings live. Their nature. How they influence living men.
4	Do you have any ideas beyond what you were taught in
5	Sunday school? I want to experience everything without
6	distinguishing between good and evil. I won't be the
7	tailor's dummy society expects me to be. I want to be a
8	noble giver of everything I've got, not the mean huckster
9	one inevitably becomes in other professions.
10	
11	
12	
13	
14	
15	
16	
17	
18	
19	
20	
21	
22	
23	
24	
25	
26	
27	
28	
29	
30	
31	
32	
33	
34	
35	

Punch Drunk
by Ethan Sandler and Josie Dickson

1   Alpha Male — Indeterminate Age   Male — Seriocomic

2

3   *The following monolog is a ladder-type of speech that*
4   *presents a long and complicated "build" to the climax*
5   *occurring very close to the final lines. It is structurally*
6   *challenging to perform it effectively, and requires a lot of*
7   *physicalization. It can also be effectively played with strong*
8   *curiosity and fascination from the outset, and a tremendous*
9   *enthusiasm for the subject. Throughout the narrative, there*
10 *are additional glimpses of other sides of this narrator's*
11 *personality that the actor can use: his admiration for his*
12 *subject, his perplexity about the dynamics of man-animal*
13 *communication, and his sarcasm towards "traditional"*
14 *clichés about primate intelligence. The actor should enjoy the*
15 *"physicalization" of the various animals, and the conflicting*
16 *emotions of weakness and intelligence. What perhaps*
17 *fascinates the narrator most of all is not the gorilla's*
18 *intelligence, but his raw power.*

19

20 When I go to the zoo I go for one reason and one reason
21 only, and that is to go to the primate house. Because
22 when you go to the primate house, they take you
23 through a very specific chain of events. They start you
24 off with the little, squirrely, quadruped monkeys that
25 scamper around. Like the one in *Raiders of the Lost Ark.*
26 "Bad date." Then they take you to the tail-swinging,
27 hooting monkeys. Gibbons and whatnot. Then they take
28 you to the baboons, the little devil-creatures with fangs
29 that curse you as you walk by. *(Baboon curse:)*

123

1   Laugssaiiisdjbb!! Then they take you to the
2   chimpanzees, the chimpanzees that have little frontal
3   lobes. Little eyelashes, hands, families. You are looking
4   into a mirror. And you could stare at the chimpanzees all
5   day if it wasn't for that hot pink, steaming pillow-ass
6   they have, which becomes intolerable after about five
7   minutes. *(Gagging)* Then you go to the gorillas. The
8   gorillas, who are e-mailing each other. The gorillas, who
9   are playing badminton. The gorillas, who have
10   committees, they take votes, and have meetings. And
11   one time I was at the Lincoln Park Zoo with a friend, and
12   we were looking at the gorilla exhibit and, as which
13   always happens when you go to the gorillas at the zoo,
14   my eyes fell on him. And he was 154 of me. He is
15   gigantic. He is this neck and these shoulders, and these
16   arms, and these hands. And this brow which could serve
17   as a cup-tray. *(Mime drinking from glass and replacing it on*
18   *brow cup-tray.)* And he sat with his back against the
19   glass, and I was with a friend. And I put my hands up
20   against the glass, driven by a desire to look him in the
21   eyes. The desire to look a giant gorilla in the eye was
22   overwhelming. And I was "Hi. Hi, Mr. Giant Man Gorilla.
23   You could eat me." And he sat there, and he looked up
24   at me. And then he looked back down at this hay he was
25   playing with — which always aggravates me when it
26   comes to gorillas because I think they should be
27   fashioning some sort of sundial. "But not me! I will get
28   to the sundial tomorrow! Today is a day to play with this
29   dead grass!" And he looks up at me and looks back
30   down at his hay. He looks up at me and he looks back
31   down at his hay. He looks up at me, scratches his arm
32   and then BOOOOOMMMMMM!! He slams his fist
33   against the glass!!! And all the other gorillas in the
34   exhibit were like "BLAH BLAH BLAH!!!" And all the
35   other primates in the building were like

1   "WHODOORIEJFASF!" And my friend was like "WHAT
2   DID YOU DO?!" And I was like "I DON'T KNOW!" And
3   he walks very calmly past the swinging tire, plants
4   himself in another corner and picks up a new batch of
5   hay. He is called the Alpha-male. There is always one of
6   him in every cage. And there is always, only one of him
7   in every cage.
8
9
10
11
12
13
14
15
16
17
18
19
20
21
22
23
24
25
26
27
28
29
30
31
32
33
34
35

Permissions Acknowledgements

A TUESDAY IN APRIL by Max Bush, © 1999 by Max Bush, is reprinted here by special arrangement of the author. All questions regarding performance royalties should be directed to Max Bush, 5372 132nd Avenue, Hamilton, Michigan 49419.

ABINGDON SQUARE by Maria Irene Fornés is reprinted by permission of Helen Merrill Ltd. on behalf of the Author. **CAUTION NOTE**: Professionals and amateurs are hereby warned that performance of *ABINGDON SQUARE* by Maria Irene Fornés is subject to a royalty. It is fully protected under the copyright laws of the United States of America, and of all countries covered by the International Copyright Union (including the Dominion of Canada and the rest of the British Commonwealth), and of all countries covered by the Pan-American Copyright Convention, the Universal Copyright Convention, the Berne Convention and of all other countries with which the United States has reciprocal copyright relations. All rights, including professional/amateur stage rights, motion picture, recitation, lecturing, public reading, radio broadcasting, television, video or sound recording, all other forms of mechanical or electronic reproduction, such as CD-ROM, CD-I, information storage and retrieval systems and photocopying, and the rights of translation into foreign languages, are strictly reserved. Particular emphasis is laid on the question of readings, permission for which must be secured from the author's agent in writing. The stage performance rights in *ABINGDON SQUARE* are controlled exclusively by Helen Merrill Ltd. No professional or non-professional performance of the play may be given without obtaining in advance the written permission of Helen Merrill Ltd., and paying the requisite fee. Inquiries concerning all rights should be addressed to Helen Merrill Ltd., 425 W. 23rd Street, 1F, New York NY 10011.

BROWN & BLACK & WHITE ALL OVER by Antonio Sacre, © 1998 by Antonio Sacre. Excerpt based upon an ancient Aztec myth, "The Rabbit in the Moon." All rights reserved. All inquiries regarding rights should be addressed to Antonio Sacre, P.O. Box 478075, Chicago IL 60647-8075.

CLEVELAND RAINING, © 1995 by Sung Rno. **CAUTION:** Professionals and amateurs are hereby warned that *CLEVELAND RAINING* is subject to a royalty. It is fully protected under the copyright laws of the United States of America and of all countries covered by the

HEAVEN'S HARD by Jordan Budde is reprinted by special arrangement with the author. All inquiries regarding rights should be addressed to the author's agent: Michael VanDyck, Major Clients Agency, 345 N. Maple Dr. #395, Beverly Hills CA 90210.

INTERBOROUGH TRANSIT by Adam Kraar. © 1998 by Adam Kraar. Reprinted by permission of the author. All inquiries regarding rights should be addressed to the author's agent, John Buzzetti, The Gersh Agency, 130 W. 42nd Street, New York NY 10036.

JAMBULU by Mary Fengar Gail. © 1999 by Mary Fengar Gail. Reprinted by permission of the author. All inquiries regarding rights should be addressed to the author at 14 Del Rey, Irvine CA 92612.

LADY LIBERTY by Adam Kraar. © 1998 by Adam Kraar. Reprinted by permission of the author. All inquiries regarding rights should be addressed to the author's agent, John Buzzetti, The Gersh Agency, 130 W. 42nd Street, New York NY 10036.

LES TROIS DUMAS by Charles Smith. © 1995 by Charles Smith. All rights reserved. Reprinted by permission. All inquiries regarding rights should be addressed to the author's agent, Barbara Hogenson, The Barbara Hogenson Agency, 165 West End Ave., Suite 19-C, New York NY 10023.

LOVE'S LABOURS WONNE by Don Nigro. Copyright © 1981 by Don Nigro. Copyright © 1995 by Don Nigro. **CAUTION:** Professionals and amateurs are hereby warned that *LOVE'S LABOURS WONNE,* being fully protected under the copyright laws of the United States of America, the British Commonwealth countries, including Canada, and the other countries of the Copyright Union, is subject to a royalty. All rights, including professional, amateur, motion picture, recitation, public reading, radio, television and cable broadcasting, and the rights of translation into foreign languages, are strictly reserved. Any inquiry regarding the availability of performance rights, or the purchase of individual copies of the authorized acting edition, must be directed to Samuel French Inc., 45 West 25th Street, New York NY 10010 with other locations in Hollywood and Toronto, Canada.

NIGHT BREATH by Dennis Clontz. Copyright © 1984 by Dennis Clontz. **CAUTION:** All rights reserved. Professionals and amateurs are hereby warned that *NIGHT BREATH* is subject to a royalty. It is fully protected under the copyright laws of the United States of America, and all countries covered by the International Copyright Union (including the Dominion of Canada and the rest of the British Commonwealth), and of

129

all countries covered by the Pan-American Copyright Convention and of all countries with which the United States has reciprocal copyright relations. All rights, including professional, amateur, motion pictures, recitation, lecturing, public reading, radio broadcasting, television, and the rights of translation into foreign languages are strictly reserved. Particular emphasis is laid upon the question of readings, permission for which must be secured from the author's representative in writing. All inquiries should be addressed to Robert A. Freedman Dramatic Agency, Inc., 1501 Broadway, Suite 2310, New York NY 10036.

NIGHTFALL WITH EDGAR ALLAN POE by Eric Coble. Copyright © 1998 by Eric Coble. All rights reserved. Reprinted by permission of the author. Inquiries regarding rights should be addressed to the author at 3011 Edgehill, Cleveland Heights OH 44118.

NIGHT LUSTER by Laura Harrington is reprinted by permission of the author. All rights reserved. Inquiries regarding rights should be addressed to the author's agent: Mary Harden, Harden-Curtis Associates, 850 7th Avenue, New York NY 10019.

NIGHT TRAIN TO BOLINA by Nilo Cruz is used by special arrangement with the author's agent, Peregrine Whittlesey, 345 East 80th Street, New York NY 10021. No performance or reading of this work may be given without express permission of the author. Inquiries regarding performance rights should be addressed to the author's agent.

PRINCIPIA SCRIPTORIAE by Richard Nelson. © 1986 by Richard Nelson. Reprinted by permission of William Morris Agency, Inc. on behalf of the Author. All rights reserved. **CAUTION:** Professionals and amateurs are hereby warned that *PRINCIPIA SCIPTORIAE* is subject to a royalty. It is fully protected under the copyright laws of the United States of America and of all countries covered by the International Copyright Union (including the Dominion of Canada and the rest of the British Commonwealth), the Berne Convention, the Pan-American Copyright Convention and the Universal Copyright Convention as well as all countries with which the United States has reciprocal copyright relations. All rights including professional/amateur stage rights, motion pictures, recitation, lecturing, public reading, radio broadcasting, television, video or sound recording, all other forms of mechanical or electronic reproduction, such as CD-ROM, CD-I, information storage and retrieval systems and photocopying, and the rights of translation into foreign languages, are strictly reserved. Particular emphasis is laid upon the matter of readings, permission for which must be secured from the

Author's agent in writing. For amateur and stock performances, please contact Broadway Play Publishing Inc., 357 West 20th Street, New York NY 10011. Inquiries concerning all other rights should be addressed to: William Morris Agency, Inc., 1325 Avenue of the Americas, New York NY 10019, Attn: Peter Franklin.

PRODIGAL KISS by Caridad Svich. © 1998 by Caridad Svich. All rights reserved. Reprinted by permission of the author. Inquiries regarding rights should be addressed to A.S.K. Theatre Projects, 11845 West Olympic Blvd., Suite #120 West, Los Angeles CA 90064.

PUNCH DRUNK by Ethan Sandler and Josie Dickson. © 1999 by Ethan Sandler and Josie Dickson. All rights reserved. Reprinted by permission of the authors. Inquiries regarding rights should be addressed to The Horrible but True Project, 334 West 49th #4FW, New York NY 10019.

PUNK GIRLS: ON DIVINE OMNIPOTENCE AND THE LONGSTANDING NATURE OF EVIL. © 1998 by Elizabeth Wong. All rights reserved. **CAUTION:** Professionals and amateurs are hereby warned that *PUNK GIRLS* is subject to a royalty. It is fully protected under the copyright laws of the United States of America and of all countries covered by the International Copyright Union (including the Dominion of Canada and the rest of the British Commonwealth), the Berne Convention, the Pan-American Copyright Convention and the Universal Copyright Convention as well as all countries with which the United States has reciprocal copyright relations. All rights including professional/amateur stage rights, motion pictures, recitation, lecturing, public reading, radio broadcasting, television, video or sound recording, all other forms of mechanical or electronic reproduction, such as CD-ROM, CD-I, information storage and retrieval systems and photocopying, and the rights of translation into foreign languages, are strictly reserved. Particular emphasis is laid upon the matter of readings, permission for which must be secured from the Author's agent in writing. All inquiries concerning rights should be addressed to: William Morris Agency, Inc., 1325 Avenue of the Americas, New York NY 10019, Attn: Jason Fogelson.

RETRO and *SEA OF FORMS* by Megan Terry are used by special arrangement with the author's agent, Tonda Marton, the Elisabeth Marton Agency, 1 Union Square West, New York NY 10003-3303. No performance or reading of this work may be given without express permission of the author. Inquiries regarding performance rights should be addressed to the author's agent.

ROUGH STOCK by Ric Averill. ©1998 by Ric Averill. All rights reserved. Inquiries regarding performance rights should be addressed to the author, 2 Winona, Lawrence KS 66046.

SALLY'S GONE, SHE LEFT HER NAME by Russell Davis. All inquiries regarding rights should be addressed to the Susan Gurman Agency, 865 West End, New York NY 10025 (212) 749-4618. Professionals and amateurs are hereby warned that performances of *SALLY'S GONE, SHE LEFT HER NAME* are subject to a royalty. It is fully protected under the copyright laws of the United States of America, and of all countries covered by the International Copyright Union (including the Dominion of Canada and the rest of the British Commonwealth), and of all countries covered by the Pan American Copyright Convention and the Universal Copyright Convention, and of all countries with which the United States has reciprocal copyright relations. All rights, including professional, amateur, motion picture, recitation, lecturing, public reading, radio broadcasting, television, video or sound taping, all other forms of mechanical or electronic reproduction, such as information storage and retrieval systems and photocopying and the rights of translation into foreign languages, are strictly reserved. Particular emphasis is laid upon the question of readings, permission for which must be secured from the author's agent in writing.

SOUVENIRS by Sheldon Rosen. All inquiries regarding rights should be addressed to the Joyce Ketay Agency, 1501 Broadway, Suite 1908, New York, NY 10036 (212) 354-6825. Professionals and amateurs are hereby warned that performances of *SOUVENIRS* are subject to a royalty. It is fully protected under the copyright laws of the United States of America, and of all countries covered by the International Copyright Union (including the Dominion of Canada and the rest of the British Commonwealth), and of all countries covered by the Pan American Copyright Convention and the Universal Copyright Convention, and of all countries with which the United States has reciprocal copyright relations. All rights, including professional, amateur, motion picture, recitation, lecturing, public reading, radio broadcasting, television, video or sound taping, all other forms of mechanical or electronic reproduction, such as information storage and retrieval systems and photocopying and the rights of translation into foreign languages, are strictly reserved. Particular emphasis is laid upon the question of readings, permission for which must be secured from the author's agent in writing.

STUCK by Adele Edling Shank is reprinted by permission of Helen Merrill Ltd. on behalf of the Author. **CAUTION NOTE:** Professionals and amateurs are hereby warned that performance of *STUCK* by Robert Shenkaan is subject to a royalty. It is fully protected under the copyright laws of the United States of America, and of all countries covered by the International Copyright Union (including the Dominion of Canada and the rest of the British Commonwealth), and of all countries covered by the Pan-American Copyright Convention, the Universal Copyright Convention, the Berne Convention and of all other countries with which the United States has reciprocal copyright relations. All rights, including professional/amateur stage rights, motion picture, recitation, lecturing, public reading, radio broadcasting, television, video or sound recording, all other forms of mechanical or electronic reproduction, such as CD-ROM, CD-I, information storage and retrieval systems and photocopying, and the rights of translation into foreign languages, are strictly reserved. Particular emphasis is laid on the question of readings, permission for which must be secured from the author's agent in writing. The stage performance rights in *STUCK* are controlled exclusively by Helen Merrill Ltd. No professional or non-professional performance of the Play may be given without obtaining in advance the written permission of Helen Merrill Ltd., and paying the requisite fee. Inquiries concerning all rights should be addressed to Helen Merrill Ltd., 425 W. 23rd Street, 1F, New York NY 10011.

SUNDAY SERMON by David Henry Hwang is reprinted by special arrangement with the author. All inquiries regarding rights should be addressed to the author's agent: William Craver, Writers and Artists Agency, 19 West 44th Street #1000, New York NY 10036.

THE BOILER ROOM by Reuben Gonzalez. © MCMXCIV by Reuben Gonzalez. Printed in the United States of America. All rights reserved. Reprinted with permission of Dramatic Publishing, 311 Washington St., Woodstock IL 60098.

THE CHINA CRISIS by Kipp Erante Cheng, © 1994 by Kipp Erante Cheng, is reprinted here by special arrangement with the author. All questions regarding performance royalties should be directed to Kipp Erante Cheng, 750 Grand St. #2A Brooklyn, NY 11211.

THE EMERALD CIRCLE by Max Bush, © MCMXCVIII by Max Bush. Printed in the United States of America. All rights reserved. Reprinted with permission of Dramatic Publishing, 311 Washington St., Woodstock IL 60098.

THE FIFTH SUN by Nicholas A. Patricca. Reprinted by special arrangement with The Dramatic Publishing Company.

locations in Hollywood and Toronto, Canada. Copyright © 1986 by John Olive. All inquiries concerning rights should be addressed to Samuel French Inc., 45 W. 25th St., New York NY 10010. No performance may be given without obtaining in advance the written permission of Samuel French Inc., and paying the requisite fee.

THE WEB by Martha Boesing. Reprinted by special permission with the author, Martha Boesing, 3144 10th Avenue South, Minneapolis MN 55407. All requests for performance rights should be addressed to the author.

THIS ONE THING I DO and *BLUE SKIES FOREVER* by Claire Braz-Valentine. Reprinted by special permission with the author, Claire Braz-Valentine, 4160 Jade St. #31, Capitola CA 95010. All requests for performance rights should be addressed to the author.

TONGUE OF A BIRD, © 1999 by Ellen McLaughlin. All inquiries regarding rights should be addressed to Joyce P. Ketay, The Joyce Ketay Agency, 1501 Broadway, Suite 1908, New York NY 10036 (212) 354-6825. Professionals and amateurs are hereby warned that performances of TONGUE OF A BIRD are subject to a royalty. It is fully protected under the copyright laws of the United States of America, and of all countries covered by the International Copyright Union (including the Dominion of Canada and the rest of the British Commonwealth), and of all countries covered by the Pan American Copyright Convention and the Universal Copyright Convention, and of all countries with which the United States has reciprocal copyright relations. All rights, including professional, amateur, motion picture, recitation, lecturing, public reading, radio broadcasting, television, video or sound taping, all other forms of mechanical or electronic reproduction, such as information storage and retrieval systems and photocopying and the rights of translation into foreign languages, are strictly reserved. Particular emphasis is laid upon the question of readings, permission for which must be secured from the author's agent in writing.

TRUTH: THE TESTIMONIAL OF SOJOURNER TRUTH by Eric Coble. Copyright © 1998 by Eric Coble. All rights reserved. Reprinted by permission of the author. Inquiries regarding rights should be addressed to the author at 3011 Edgehill, Cleveland Heights OH 44118.

WETTER THAN WATER by Deborah Pryor is reprinted by special arrangement with the author. All inquiries regarding rights should be addressed to the author's agent: William Craver, Wrters and Artists Agency, 19 West 44th Street Suite #10000, New York NY 10036.

WHEN THE BOUGH BREAKS by Robert Clyman is reprinted by permission of Helen Merrill Ltd. on behalf of the Author. **CAUTION NOTE:** Professionals and amateurs are hereby warned that performance of *WHEN THE BOUGH BREAKS* by Robert Clyman is subject to a royalty. It is fully protected under the copyright laws of the United States of America, and of all countries covered by the International Copyright Union (including the Dominion of Canada and the rest of the British Commonwealth), and of all countries covered by the Pan-American Copyright Convention, the Universal Copyright Convention, the Berne Convention and of all other countries with which the United States has reciprocal copyright relations. All rights, including professional/amateur stage rights, motion picture, recitation, lecturing, public reading, radio broadcasting, television, video or sound recording, all other forms of mechanical or electronic reproduction, such as CD-ROM, CD-I, information storage and retrieval systems and photocopying, and the rights of translation into foreign languages, are strictly reserved. Particular emphasis is laid on the question of readings, permission for which must be secured from the author's agent in writing. The stage performance rights in *WHEN THE BOUGH BREAKS* are controlled exclusively by Helen Merrill Ltd. No professional or non-professional performance of the play may be given without obtaining in advance the written permission of Helen Merrill Ltd., and paying the requisite fee. Inquiries concerning all rights should be addressed to Helen Merrill Ltd., 425 W. 23rd Street, 1F, New York NY 10011.

WHO EVER SAID I WAS A GOOD GIRL? By Gustavo Ott, translated by Heather McKay. ©1996 by Gustavo Ott, all rights reserved. Reprinted by permission. Information concerning rights should be addressed to the author: Gustavo Ott, Apartado Postal 4945, Carmelitas 1010, Caracas, Venezuela.

About the Editor

Roger Ellis earned his M.A. in English and Drama from the University of Santa Clara, and his Ph.D. in Dramatic Art from the University of California at Berkeley. During that time he was also guest stage director for several colleges and universities. He has authored or edited eight books in theatre, plus numerous articles, essays and short stories. In 1991 he initiated an ethnic theatre program at Grand Valley State University in Michigan, creating guest artist residencies and staging plays celebrating cultural diversity; and he has been director of the University's Shakespeare Festival since 1993. He has worked professionally as actor or director with various Michigan and California theatres; and has served as President of the Theatre Alliance of Michigan for the past six years. He often serves as an adjudicator for high school forensics and thespian activities, and frequently conducts workshops in acting and auditioning skills for high schools and universities. He is currently a Professor of Theatre at Grand Valley State University.